D0376421

THE
QUICK AND EASY
VEGETARIAN
COLLEGE
COOKBOOK

300
HEALTHY, LOW-COST MEALS THAT FIT YOUR BUDGET AND SCHEDULE

Adams Media
New York   London   Toronto   Sydney   New Delhi

Adams Media
An Imprint of Simon & Schuster, Inc.
57 Littlefield Street
Avon, Massachusetts 02322

First Adams Media trade paperback edition JULY 2017

ADAMS MEDIA and colophon are trademarks of Simon and Schuster.

For information about special discounts for bulk purchases, please contact Simon & Schuster Special Sales at 1-866-506-1949 or business@simonandschuster.com.

The Simon & Schuster Speakers Bureau can bring authors to your live event. For more information or to book an event contact the Simon & Schuster Speakers Bureau at 1-866-248-3049 or visit our website at www.simonspeakers.com.

Interior design by Heather McKiel
Interior image of dish, fork, and knife © iStockphoto.com/Icon_Craft_Studio

Manufactured in the United States of America

10 9 8 7 6 5 4 3 2 1

Library of Congress Cataloging-in-Publication Data has been applied for.

ISBN 978-1-5072-0419-1
ISBN 978-1-5072-0420-7 (ebook)

Contains material adapted from the following titles published by Adams Media, an Imprint of Simon & Schuster, Inc.: *The Everything® Easy Vegetarian Cookbook* by Jay Weinstein, copyright © 2015, ISBN 978-1-4405-8719-1; *The Everything® Eating Clean Cookbook for Vegetarians* by Britt Brandon, copyright © 2013, ISBN 978-1-4405-5140-6; *The Everything® Vegan Baking Cookbook* by Lorena Novak Bull, copyright © 2012, ISBN 978-1-4405-2997-9; *The Everything® Healthy College Cookbook* by Nicole Cormier, copyright © 2010, ISBN 978-1-4405-0411-2; *The Everything® Vegetarian Cookbook* by Jay Weinstein, copyright © 2002, ISBN 978-1-58062-640-8; and *The Quick and Easy College Cookbook*, copyright © 2016, ISBN 978-1-4405-9523-3.

CONTENTS

INTRODUCTION

Welcome to college! A time for fun, learning, and, yes, amazing vegetarian food. It's true. The days when vegetarians suffered through overcooked rice dishes and flavorless veggie burgers prepared by their college dining halls are long gone. Now you can whip up a batch of Pumpkin Muffins to grab on your way to class, impress your roommates (vegetarian or not!) with Spinach and Feta Pie, or indulge a late-night sweet tooth with Triple-Chocolate Cupcakes.

These simple recipes, and the hundreds of others that you'll find throughout *The Quick and Easy Vegetarian College Cookbook*, are guaranteed to get you through your college years with your taste buds (and your wallet) intact. And by doing your own cooking, you decide what you eat and when!

If you're looking for something healthy after a busy weekend, try the Lentil-Vegetable Soup or the Tangy Three-Bean Salad. If you need something fast to whip up between classes, try the Quick Tomato and Oregano Sauté or the Scrambled Egg Burritos. If you need something to snack on as you pull yet another an all nighter, just reach for the Mini Goat Cheese Pizzas, Greek Salad Tacos, or amazing veggie French Fries.

And, if you haven't spent much time in the kitchen, don't worry. We've got your back. Many of these quick and easy recipes can be made in the toaster oven, microwave, or slow cooker, and you'll find a list of basic ingredients and equipment in Chapter 1 to get you started.

So whether you're a full-time vegetarian who is just learning how to cook or are just looking for something new and delicious to try on Meatless Monday, it's time to give cooking a try. After all, what is college if not a time to try something new!

WHAT YOU'LL NEED IN YOUR KITCHEN

Leaving home for college presents challenges as well as opportunities. For students whose kitchen know-how doesn't extend beyond the reheat setting on the microwave, the idea of having to learn basic cooking skills along with calculus can seem overwhelming. It's all too easy to give in to the lure of the dining hall or food court. However, these basic tips will help turn cooking from a chore into a creative, stress-free break from studying.

Stocking the Kitchen

There are a few basic pieces of equipment that every well-equipped kitchen should have. Of course, whether or not you bring all of them to college will depend on your specific circumstances. For example, residences with communal kitchens often provide pots, pans, and other cooking essentials for residents. And there is no point in bringing a heavy-duty frying pan if you're going to be relying on a microwave oven as your primary heat source.

Here is a basic list of items for setting up a kitchen, which you can add to or subtract from based on your own needs. Fortunately, most are quite inexpensive and can frequently be found at discount stores. Items you absolutely need for cooking include:

- Plastic mixing bowls for mixing ingredients and serving noodle and salad dishes
- Wooden spoons for stirring and mixing
- Heatproof rubber spatula for mixing ingredients and turning food during cooking
- Plastic or metal colander for draining washed, blanched, and boiled food
- Knives, particularly a good French knife for cutting fruits and vegetables
- Plastic or wooden cutting board for cutting, chopping, and mincing food
- Measuring spoons and a plastic measuring cup
- Vegetable peeler
- Can opener
- Grater for grating, shredding, and slicing cheese and other foods
- Pastry brush for basting food
- Wire whisk for whisking sauces and eggs

Mix It Up!

Many recipes call for food to be beaten, blended, whipped, processed, or crushed. If your budget is limited, hand tools can perform many of these functions. For example, an egg beater (also called a hand mixer) is fine for beating eggs and whipping cream. And nothing beats a mortar and pestle for grinding and crushing nuts, herbs, spices, crackers, soft fruit, and almost any food that will fit into the bowl-shaped mortar.

However, if your budget permits, you may want to explore some higher-tech options for blending and mixing. The ultimate timesaving device, a blender is perfect for harried but health-conscious students. Compact, inexpensive, and easy to clean, a blender will do everything from liquefying smoothie ingredients to puréeing vegetables. Even if your cooking requirements don't extend beyond hastily throwing together breakfast on busy weekdays, a blender will help you put together a tasty and nutritious meal in mere minutes. (You may have to drink it while walking to class, but that's okay!)

BLENDER OR FOOD PROCESSOR?

Besides the basic blender, another option for mixing food is a food processor. A food processor performs all of the functions of a blender and more. Besides grating cheese and making pastry dough, higher-end models can even be used to make bread dough. However, for most students, these extra options don't justify the food processor's higher-end price tag. Furthermore, the blender's tall shape means it can hold more liquid, which makes it a better choice for preparing smoothies and other drinks. If you have the space and can afford it, a food processor is a useful addition to your kitchen, but not essential.

Electrical Extras

Some college residences allow students to keep small electrical appliances in the dorm or the residence kitchen. A coffeemaker allows you to have a cup of java ready as soon as you wake up in the morning. Tea drinkers will want a kettle for boiling water. Along with a toaster or toaster oven, these items will help make your living quarters seem more like home.

When it comes to larger appliances, definitely consider a microwave oven or a hot plate if your budget and college regulations permit it. Basically, a hot plate performs all the functions of a stovetop heating element while taking up considerably less space than a conventional stove. A hot plate can be used for everything from cooking soup to frying pork chops. Although it can't completely replace a standard electric oven, a microwave oven can be used for everything from making popcorn and reheating leftovers to preparing an entire meal. Today, compact microwave and refrigerator combinations, designed specifically for dormitories, are available. Some even come with a small freezer attached.

Another handy device for dorm cooking is a rice cooker/steamer combination. Compact and inexpensive, this appliance steams vegetables, and it cooks rice and beans more quickly than the standard stovetop heating element. As an added bonus, it has a plastic surface that makes cleaning easy. For students who have a microwave, the addition of a rice cooker/steamer can provide some of the advantages of stovetop cooking, making it unnecessary to purchase a hot plate.

Equipment for the Stovetop

A few good pots are essential for stovetop cooking. Ideally, you should have three different sizes: a smaller pot for sauces, a medium-sized pot for soups and single-serving meals, and a large pot for boiling noodles, potatoes, and cooking for a group. However, if money is an issue, it's better to purchase one pot made of quality material rather than several inexpensive pots that may not heat properly or may be hard to clean. In that case, a medium-sized pot is the most practical choice.

Make sure the saucepan is made of a heavy material that conducts heat evenly. While cast-iron and copper pots are heavier than you need (and probably beyond your budget), stainless steel wrapped in aluminum or copper is a good choice. While you can always wear oven mitts, cooking will be easier if the handles are made of a material such as wood, plastic, or rubber that won't heat up during cooking. Finally, test the lid to make sure it fits tightly.

Not surprisingly, quality frying pans are made of the same type of material as saucepans because both are designed for stovetop cooking. A medium-sized

(12") frying pan will meet all your needs for sautéing vegetables and cooking eggs. As with a saucepan, it's important to make sure the frying pan comes with a tight-fitting lid.

Oven Cooking

Oven cooking requires its own special equipment that can take the high heats needed for baking, broiling, and roasting. A large, rectangular-shaped metal baking sheet is used for making cookies, while a square, deep-sided metal baking pan is used for baking bars and desserts. When it comes to muffins, there is no substitute for a standard muffin pan—consider getting more than one to prevent having to cook in batches. A glass baking dish is used for main dishes. Finally, a deep-sided casserole dish is used for one-pot meals such as rice- and noodle-based casseroles.

Kitchen Staples

Once you've purchased the basic tools needed for cooking, it's tempting to start filling up the refrigerator. Hold off until you've purchased a few dry staple ingredients. A pantry stocked with basic ingredients—such as flour—will keep you from having to make repeat emergency trips to the local grocery store every time you cook a meal. Here are the essentials:

- ○ **Flour:** As its name implies, all-purpose flour is used for almost every type of baking.
- ○ **Sugar:** Regular granulated white sugar is used both as a sweetener at the table and in cooking.
- ○ **Brown sugar:** Molasses-based brown sugar is used in baking, sauces, and wherever a recipe calls for a stronger flavoring agent than granulated sugar.
- ○ **Olive oil:** Olive oil is used for sautéing and frying, and as a salad dressing and in marinades.
- ○ **Instant broth:** Vegetable broth is used in vegetarian soups, casseroles, and other dishes.

- O **Dried herbs and spices:** Dried herbs and spices lend flavor to soups, stews, and other slow-cooked dishes.
- O **Salt and pepper:** Standard table salt should meet all your cooking needs, but you may want to consider purchasing a pepper mill to grind your own peppercorns.
- O **Noodles:** No, they don't need to be ramen! Italian pasta noodles like linguine, penne, or even standard spaghetti are a quick and easy source of protein.
- O **Rice:** For variety, experiment with different types such as brown and scented rice.
- O **Miscellaneous flavoring agents:** Lemon juice, tomato sauce, and soy sauce will allow you to create a number of different dishes.

USE OLIVE OIL

Not only is olive oil healthier than vegetable oil—scientists believe its monounsaturated fats can help ward off heart disease—it's also much more versatile. Besides being an excellent cooking oil, olive oil lends a delicate flavor to salad dressings and marinades, and can even serve as a low-fat substitute for butter on toasted bread.

Timesaving Ingredients

While nothing beats the flavor of fresh herbs or vegetable broth prepared from scratch, packaged and instant ingredients will save you time on busy weeknights. For example, don't let recipes that call for lemon juice put you off—most supermarkets carry lemon juice in a handy plastic lemon-shaped container. Made with oregano, basil, and other seasonings, canned tomato sauce saves you from the work of having to boil and crush tomatoes. Stored in a cool, dry place, a can of unopened tomato sauce will keep for several months. (There's also a recipe in this book for Quick Tomato Sauce if you'd like to make your own but don't want to spend a lot of time on it.)

Instant vegetable broth comes in many forms, including cubes, powdered mix, cans, and ready-to-use cartons. All are equally convenient. However, the carton types need to be refrigerated and used within two weeks after they are opened.

When it comes to noodles, many types of Asian noodles—such as rice noodles—don't even need to be boiled. Just soak them in hot or warm water until they soften. And precooked (also called "oven-ready") lasagna noodles can go straight from the package to the frying pan or casserole dish.

WHICH DRIED SPICES?

There are literally hundreds of spices. However, for those on a limited budget, a good tip is to think Italian. Nothing beats dried oregano, basil, and parsley for bringing out the flavor of simmered and slow-cooked dishes. Garlic powder and onion powder make a convenient substitute for actual onion and garlic on nights that you don't feel up to peeling, mincing, and chopping.

Shelf Life

Even dry ingredients go stale eventually. Expect flour, baking powder, and baking soda to last for up to one year. White granulated sugar has a longer shelf life than other dry ingredients—it will last up to eighteen months. On the other hand, brown sugar lasts for only six months. Of course, improper storage will cause ingredients to go stale more quickly. Worse, certain types of small bugs—such as the flour beetle—feed on dry ingredients. For best results, store your staples in tightly sealed canisters.

Don't worry about blowing your budget on a matching set of fancy chrome or other metal canisters. Plastic is fine, as long as it has a tight seal. Don't have room in your dorm for a full set of canisters? Set one canister aside to serve as a storage space for smaller amounts of various ingredients. Store each ingredient in a plastic bag, seal it, and place the bag in the canister.

Meal Planning 101

Preparing a detailed grocery list makes it much easier to stick to a budget. But where do you begin? The best way is to start by preparing a meal plan for one or two weeks. Try to pick more than one recipe that uses the same ingredients so that you can save money by purchasing in bulk. Let's say, for example, that you decide to cook the Peck of Peppers Tart and Vegetarian

Lasagna. Including both recipes in the same grocery shopping trip lets you purchase larger portions of everything from peppers to onions.

Of course, you'll want to incorporate leftovers into your meal plan. But refrigerated leftovers have to be eaten within days, and eating the same meal twice in one week can get a little boring. Fortunately, there are ways around this problem.

For recipes designed to provide two or more servings, one option is to cook two half-portions of the recipe, slightly altering the ingredients for each half. When halving or doubling a recipe, it's helpful to know how to convert cups into tablespoons, tablespoons into teaspoons, and vice versa. The following table contains several conversions.

EQUIVALENT MEASURES	
Measurement	**Equivalent Measure**
3 teaspoons	1 tablespoon
4 tablespoons	¼ cup
5 tablespoons plus 1 teaspoon	⅓ cup
8 tablespoons	½ cup
10 tablespoons plus 2 teaspoons	⅓ cup
12 tablespoons	¾ cup
16 tablespoons	1 cup
48 teaspoons	1 cup
1 cup	8 ounces
1 quart	32 ounces

Shopping Tips

When writing up a grocery list, many people find it helps to organize ingredients in the same way that items are organized in the grocery store. Fresh vegetables are categorized together, as are canned vegetables and frozen foods. Items located at either end of the store are either first or last on the list. Organizing the grocery list in this way ensures that you're moving in an organized fashion from one end of the store to the other, instead of wandering back and forth between aisles.

Here are a few tips for cutting costs at the grocery store:

○ Never shop when you're tired or hungry. This makes it easier to avoid expensive "impulse buying."
○ Always bring a list and stick to it.
○ Check the "sell by" and "use by" dates on perishable items such as milk and eggs. Always purchase food with the most recent date so that it will last longer.
○ Be sure to ask for a rain check if the store is out of an advertised special.
○ Always store perishable goods in the refrigerator or freezer as soon as possible so there is no danger of spoilage.
○ Many larger supermarkets have frequent-shopper programs that give substantial discounts to regular customers. Check to see if you are eligible for a frequent-shopper card.

The Freshman Weight Gain

Statistics show that approximately half of all students put on between ten and fifteen pounds during their first year of college and university. It's easy to fall victim to the "Freshman 15" when you're living on your own for the first time, trying to adjust to a busy schedule, and fast-food vendors are scattered across campus. However, putting on weight will just increase the stress that you're already feeling from academic pressures, and it can be hard to take off later.

The benefits of a vigorous exercise session go beyond the calories expended during the workout. Exercising increases the body's metabolic rate, causing you to burn up calories at a faster rate even after you've finished your workout. The effect can last for up to two full days.

Here are a few tips for keeping the pounds away: First and foremost, stick to a regular meal schedule. If you are planning a lengthy study session away from the dorm, prepare healthy snacks to take with you. Simple snacks such as granola bars, cheese and crackers, and trail mix all provide energy without the fat and calories in potato chips and chocolate.

Plan your meals at least one week in advance. One option is to cook ahead, making all your weekly meals on the weekend. It's much easier to stick to a healthy meal plan on a busy weeknight when all you need to do is heat up dinner instead of cooking it. Finally, take time to exercise. Many colleges and universities have excellent exercise facilities right on campus that are free for students. With a little planning, you can fit an exercise session into your daily schedule. A daily swim or aerobics workout makes it easier to control your weight, and it also lifts your spirits by releasing endorphins, giving you a much-needed boost of energy.

BREAKFAST AND BREADS

Banana–Chocolate Chip Muffins

▶ MAKES 18 MUFFINS

½ cup soymilk
1 teaspoon lemon juice
¾ cup brown sugar
½ cup softened vegan margarine
3 medium bananas, mashed
1 teaspoon vanilla extract
2¼ cups all-purpose flour
1 cup whole-wheat flour
½ teaspoon baking powder
½ teaspoon baking soda
¼ teaspoon salt
1 cup coarsely chopped vegan chocolate chips
½ cup chopped walnuts (optional)

1. Preheat oven to 350°F.

2. Stir soymilk and lemon juice together in a small bowl and allow to sit 10 minutes. Cream brown sugar and margarine together in a large bowl until fluffy. Stir in bananas, vanilla, and soymilk mixture until blended.

3. In a separate bowl, whisk together flours, baking powder, baking soda, and salt. Add flour mixture to wet ingredients, stirring until just mixed. Fold in chocolate chips and optional walnuts. Fill greased or paper-lined muffin tins with batter up to ⅔ full.

4. Bake muffins 20–25 minutes or until a toothpick comes out clean when inserted into the center of a muffin. Cool in the pan 10 minutes, then transfer to wire racks. Cool completely.

Apricot-Walnut Bread

▶ SERVES 12

1 cup dried chopped apricots

⅓ cup orange juice

¼ cup brown sugar

¼ cup canola oil

¾ cup soymilk

1 teaspoon vanilla extract

2 cups all-purpose flour

1 tablespoon baking powder

½ teaspoon baking soda

½ teaspoon salt

1 cup chopped walnuts

1. Preheat oven to 350°F.

2. Combine apricots and orange juice in a small saucepan over medium-low heat and simmer 5–10 minutes until apricots are soft. Remove from heat and allow to cool. Drain apricots, reserving juice.

3. In a large bowl, whisk together reserved juice, brown sugar, oil, soymilk, and vanilla. In a medium bowl, whisk together flour, baking powder, baking soda, and salt. Add flour mixture to wet ingredients, stirring until just mixed. Fold in apricots and walnuts.

4. Pour batter evenly into a greased 9" × 5" loaf pan.

5. Bake 45–55 minutes or until golden brown and a toothpick comes out clean when inserted into the center of the loaf.

Cranberry-Orange Muffins

▶ MAKES ABOUT 20 MUFFINS

⅓ cup canola oil

⅔ cup orange juice

Egg replacement equal to 1 egg

⅓ cup soymilk

½ teaspoon vanilla extract

2 cups all-purpose flour

½ cup sugar

½ cup brown sugar

2 teaspoons baking powder

2 tablespoons orange zest

1 cup coarsely chopped fresh
   cranberries

REHYDRATING CRANBERRIES

Rehydrate your dried cranberries first in juice. Simply cover them with apple, orange, or even pineapple juice and allow them to sit until fat and plumped, about 15 minutes. If you want to get fancy, use a fruit liqueur instead of juice for a subtly gourmet flavor.

1. Preheat oven to 375°F.

2. In a large bowl, whisk together oil, orange juice, egg replacement, soymilk, and vanilla. In a separate bowl, stir together flour, sugar, brown sugar, and baking powder. Add flour mixture to wet ingredients, stirring until just mixed.

3. Gently fold in orange zest and cranberries. Pour batter ⅔ full into greased or paper-lined muffin tins.

4. Bake 20–22 minutes or until a toothpick comes out clean when inserted into the center of the muffins.

Spiced Apple Muffins

1 cup soymilk
4 tablespoons vegan margarine
Egg replacement equal to 1 egg
1 teaspoon vanilla extract
2 cups all-purpose flour
½ cup sugar
4 teaspoons baking powder
½ teaspoon salt
¾ teaspoon ground cinnamon
¼ teaspoon ground nutmeg
1 cup diced apples
Additional sugar and cinnamon for topping (optional)

1. Preheat oven to 425°F.
2. Whisk soymilk, margarine, egg replacement, and vanilla in a large bowl. In a separate bowl, whisk together flour, sugar, baking powder, salt, cinnamon, and nutmeg. Gradually combine flour mixture with wet ingredients, stirring until well mixed. Fold in apples.
3. Spoon batter into greased or paper-lined muffin tins ⅔ full. Sprinkle with additional cinnamon and sugar, if desired.
4. Bake 15–18 minutes or until a toothpick comes out clean when inserted into the center of the muffins.

Zucchini Bread

▶ SERVES 12

1½ cups all-purpose flour
1 teaspoon baking powder
1 teaspoon baking soda
½ teaspoon salt
2 teaspoons ground cinnamon
½ teaspoon ground nutmeg
1 cup sugar
½ cup canola oil
Egg replacement equal to 2 eggs
1 teaspoon vanilla extract
1 cup grated zucchini

1. Preheat oven to 350°F.

2. Whisk together flour, baking powder, baking soda, salt, cinnamon, and nutmeg in a large bowl. In a separate bowl, stir together sugar, oil, egg replacement, and vanilla. Add wet ingredients to flour mixture, stirring until just mixed. Fold in grated zucchini.

3. Pour batter into a greased loaf pan and bake 50–60 minutes until golden brown. A toothpick should come out clean when inserted into the center of the loaf. Cool in the pan.

VEGGIE BREADS

Like most recipes, zucchini bread can be embellished with additional ingredients. Dried fruits and nuts are nice and add a touch of sweetness and a pleasant crunch. This bread also stands up well to a variety of vegetable additions. Try grating in a mixture of carrots, yellow squash, and red bell peppers for a bread that looks like a slice of confetti. You can add up to an additional 1½ cups of extra ingredients.

Corn Bread

▶ SERVES 12

1 cup all-purpose flour
1 cup yellow cornmeal
¾ cup sugar
2½ teaspoons baking powder
1 teaspoon salt
Egg replacement equal to 2 eggs
1 cup soymilk
½ cup canola oil

1. Preheat oven to 400°F.
2. Combine flour, cornmeal, sugar, baking powder, and salt in a large bowl. In a separate bowl, mix egg replacement, soymilk, and oil. Add wet ingredients to flour mixture, stirring until just mixed. Pour batter into a greased 8" × 8" pan.
3. Bake 20–25 minutes or until a toothpick comes out clean when inserted into the center of the bread and the top is golden brown.

REUSE AND RECYCLE!

Recycle this basic recipe by adding an extra garnish or two each time you make it: a touch of fresh rosemary, a couple of shakes of a vegan Parmesan cheese, some chopped toasted nuts or vegetarian bacon bits for crunch. For a Thanksgiving side dish, toss in some rehydrated dried cranberries.

Maple-Oat Muffins

⅔ cup cold cooked oatmeal

Egg replacement equal to 1 egg

2 tablespoons canola oil

¼ cup Grade B maple syrup

¾ cup soymilk

2 cups all-purpose flour

3 teaspoons baking powder

2 tablespoons sugar

½ teaspoon salt

1. Preheat oven to 425°F.
2. Stir together oatmeal, egg replacement, oil, maple syrup, and soymilk in a large bowl until blended. In a separate bowl, whisk together flour, baking powder, sugar, and salt. Combine flour mixture with wet ingredients, stirring until just mixed.
3. Pour batter into greased or paper-lined muffin tins ⅔ full. Bake 20–25 minutes or until a toothpick inserted into the center comes out clean.

Pumpkin Muffins

▶ MAKES ABOUT 20 MUFFINS

1½ cups all-purpose flour

1 cup whole-wheat flour

¾ cup sugar

1 tablespoon baking powder

½ teaspoon baking soda

½ teaspoon salt

1 teaspoon ground cinnamon

½ teaspoon ground nutmeg

¼ teaspoon ground ginger

¼ teaspoon ground allspice

1 (15-ounce) can pumpkin purée

¼ cup canola oil

¼ cup soymilk

Egg replacement equal to 1 egg

½ teaspoon minced lemon zest

½ cup raisins

DITCH THE CAN

If you've got the time, there's nothing like fresh roasted pumpkin! Make your own purée to substitute for canned. Carefully chop your pumpkin in half, remove the seeds (save and toast those later!), and place cut-side down in a large baking dish. Pour ¼" water into the bottom of the dish and roast 45–60 minutes in a 375°F oven. Cool, then peel off and discard the skin. Mash or purée the flesh until smooth. Whatever you don't use will keep in the freezer for next time.

1. Preheat oven to 375°F.

2. In a large bowl, combine all-purpose flour, whole-wheat flour, sugar, baking powder, baking soda, salt, cinnamon, nutmeg, ginger, and allspice. In a separate bowl, mix pumpkin purée, oil, soymilk, egg replacement, and lemon zest. Add to flour mixture, stirring until just mixed. Fold in raisins.

3. Pour batter into greased or paper-lined muffin tins ⅔ full.

4. Bake 25–35 minutes or until a toothpick inserted into the center of the muffins comes out clean. Remove from pan to cool.

Boston Brown Bread

2 cups soymilk, less 2 tablespoons
2 tablespoons apple cider vinegar
1 cup all-purpose flour
2 cups whole-wheat flour
2 teaspoons baking soda
⅔ cup packed brown sugar
¼ cup molasses
½ cup raisins

1. Preheat oven to 350°F.
2. Combine soymilk and vinegar in a small bowl and allow to sit 10 minutes.
3. In a large bowl, combine all-purpose flour, whole-wheat flour, baking soda, and brown sugar. Stir in molasses and soymilk mixture until just combined. Fold in raisins.
4. Pour batter into a greased and floured 9" × 5" loaf pan and bake 55–60 minutes. Remove from pan to cool.

Blueberry Crumb Muffins

2¾ cups all-purpose flour, divided

1½ cups sugar, divided

1 tablespoon baking powder

½ teaspoon salt

¼ cup softened vegan margarine

½ cup unsweetened applesauce

½ cup soymilk

1 teaspoon vanilla extract

1½ cups frozen blueberries

⅓ cup cold and diced vegan margarine

1. Preheat oven to 350°F.

2. Combine 2 cups flour, 1 cup sugar, baking powder, and salt in a large bowl. In a separate bowl, mix softened margarine, applesauce, soymilk, and vanilla until blended. Fold in frozen blueberries. Pour batter into greased or paper-lined muffin tins ¾ full.

3. In a small bowl, combine remaining ¾ cup flour and ½ cup sugar. Cut cold margarine into flour and sugar until mixture is crumbly. Sprinkle mixture over the top of muffin batter.

4. Bake 30–35 minutes or until a toothpick comes out clean when inserted into center of the muffins.

Simple Cloverleaf Dinner Rolls

▶ SERVES 12

1 envelope active dry yeast
3 tablespoons lukewarm water
1 cup lukewarm milk (about 110°F)
6 tablespoons butter, divided
3 tablespoons sugar
1 large egg
1 teaspoon salt
3½–4 cups all-purpose flour
Few drops vegetable oil

1. In a large mixing bowl, combine yeast with 3 tablespoons lukewarm water. Let stand 5 minutes. Add milk, 4 tablespoons butter, sugar, egg, and salt; mix well with a wooden spoon. Gradually add 2 cups flour; mix 1 minute. Gradually mix in 1½–2 cups more flour until dough is moist but not sticky. Knead 10 minutes until dough is smooth and elastic. Form into a ball and place in a mixing bowl with a few drops of oil; toss to coat. Cover bowl with plastic wrap; allow to rise in a warm place until double in size, 1–1½ hours. Knead dough 1 minute; cover and refrigerate 30 minutes.

2. Form into 36 tight, round balls, rolling them against an unfloured surface. In a buttered muffin tin, place 3 balls in each muffin cup; cover loosely with greased plastic wrap. Allow to rise in a warm place until double in size, 1–1½ hours.

3. Preheat oven to 375°F. Melt remaining 3 tablespoons butter and brush it onto the rolls. Bake 25–30 minutes until golden brown.

Date-Nut Loaf

▶ SERVES 16

½ cup packed brown sugar
½ cup softened vegan margarine
1 cup water
1 teaspoon vanilla extract
2 cups all-purpose flour
2 teaspoons baking powder
1 teaspoon baking soda
¼ teaspoon salt
1 cup pitted, chopped dates
½ cup chopped walnuts

1. Preheat oven to 400°F.

2. In a large bowl, cream brown sugar and margarine together until fluffy. Mix in water and vanilla. In a separate bowl, whisk together flour, baking powder, baking soda, and salt. Add flour mixture to margarine mixture, stirring until just blended. Fold in chopped dates and nuts.

3. Pour batter into a greased 9" × 5" loaf pan. Bake 40–45 minutes or until golden brown and a toothpick comes out clean when inserted into the center of the loaf. Cool in the pan.

Banana Bread

▶ SERVES 12

3 ripe bananas, mashed
½ cup sugar
¼ cup packed brown sugar
Egg replacement equal to 2 eggs
1 teaspoon vanilla extract
1½ cups all-purpose flour
½ cup whole-wheat flour
1 teaspoon baking soda
1 teaspoon salt
½ cup chopped walnuts (optional)

BAKING WITH BANANAS

The best bananas for baking are overripe and black. Their starch has completely converted to sugar, which makes them awful to eat fresh, but perfectly moist and sweet for baking. If your bananas are headed in that direction but you don't have time to bake, remove them from their skin, place them in a plastic zipper bag, smash them up a little, and store in the freezer. They'll be ready at a moment's notice for your next banana bake-off.

1. Preheat oven to 350°F.

2. In a large bowl, stir together mashed bananas, sugar, brown sugar, egg replacement, and vanilla until well blended. In a separate bowl, combine the flours, baking soda, and salt. Add flour mixture to wet ingredients, stirring until just mixed. Fold in walnuts if desired.

3. Pour batter into a greased 9" × 5" loaf pan and bake 1 hour or until top is golden brown and a toothpick comes out clean when inserted into the center of the loaf. Cool in the pan.

Beer Bread

▶ SERVES 16

2 cups all-purpose flour
1 cup whole-wheat flour
1 tablespoon baking powder
¼ cup sugar
1½ teaspoons salt
12 ounces beer
3 tablespoons melted vegan margarine

1. Preheat oven to 375°F.
2. In a large bowl, whisk together all-purpose flour, whole-wheat flour, baking powder, sugar, and salt. Stir in beer until just mixed. Spread dough in a greased 9" × 5" loaf pan. Brush top of dough with melted margarine.
3. Bake 40–45 minutes or until a toothpick comes out clean when inserted into the center of the loaf and the top is golden brown.

Lemon Bread

▶ SERVES 16

2 cups all-purpose flour
2 teaspoons baking powder
¼ teaspoon salt
½ cup vegetable shortening
1 cup sugar
4 tablespoons lemon juice, divided
2 tablespoons minced lemon zest
Egg replacement equal to 2 eggs
1 teaspoon vanilla extract
½ cup soymilk
½ cup confectioners' sugar

QUICK BAKING

Quick breads are so named because they are leavened with baking powder and/or baking soda, which do not require the prolonged fermentation time that yeast does. However, quick breads are not necessarily quick to bake. Batters baked in a loaf pan require time to allow heat to penetrate to the center. Regardless of the indicated baking time, the toothpick test is the only true measure of doneness. When inserted, it must come out clean.

1. Preheat oven to 350°F.

2. In a medium bowl, whisk together the flour, baking powder, and salt. Set aside. In a large bowl, cream the shortening and sugar until fluffy. Add 2 tablespoons lemon juice, lemon zest, egg replacement, and vanilla; whisk until well blended.

3. Add the flour mixture to the wet ingredients alternating with the soymilk, stirring until just mixed. Pour batter into a greased 8" × 4" loaf pan and bake 45–50 minutes or until a toothpick comes out clean when inserted into the center.

4. In a small bowl, combine the remaining 2 tablespoons lemon juice and the confectioners' sugar to create a glaze.

5. Remove bread from pan and while still warm drizzle with lemon glaze.

Southwest Green Chile Corn Muffins

▶ MAKES 16 MUFFINS

¼ cup vegetable shortening
¼ cup sugar
1 cup soymilk
Egg replacement equal to 1 egg
½ cup cream-style corn
1 (4-ounce) can diced green chilies, drained
1 cup cornmeal
1 cup all-purpose flour
4 teaspoons baking powder
½ teaspoon salt

1. Preheat oven to 375°F.
2. In a large bowl, cream shortening and sugar until fluffy. Add soymilk, egg replacement, cream-style corn, and green chilies. Stir to combine. In a separate bowl, whisk together cornmeal, flour, baking powder, and salt. Add flour mixture to wet ingredients, stirring until just mixed.
3. Pour batter into greased or paper-lined muffin tins ⅔ full. Bake 15–20 minutes or until a toothpick comes out clean when inserted into the center of the muffins and the tops are lightly browned.

Spicy Southwestern Corn Bread

▶ MAKES 2 LOAVES

4½ cups fine cornmeal

1 cup sugar

2 cups flour

4 tablespoons baking powder

1 tablespoon baking soda

4 teaspoons table salt

3½ cups buttermilk

1 cup canola oil

1 cup (2 sticks) melted butter

6 eggs

1½ tablespoons chopped jalapeño peppers

2 tablespoons puréed chipotle in adobo

1. Preheat oven to 400°F. In a large mixing bowl, combine the cornmeal, sugar, flour, baking powder, baking soda, and salt. Mix thoroughly with a stiff wire whisk or spoon to combine well and break up any lumps. In a separate mixing bowl, mix the buttermilk, oil, melted butter, eggs, jalapeños, and chipotle; whisk well to combine. Fold the cornmeal mixture into the buttermilk mixture in three additions, mixing only as much as necessary to combine ingredients. Pour the batter into two 9" × 5" loaf pans or one 9" × 13" baking dish. It is not necessary to grease the pans.

2. Bake until the top springs back when pressed and a toothpick comes out clean when inserted into the center, about 30 minutes. Cool 10 minutes in the pan before turning onto a rack to cool completely.

Carrot-Raisin Muffins

▶ MAKES 16 MUFFINS

2 cups all-purpose flour
¼ teaspoon salt
1 teaspoon baking powder
¼ teaspoon baking soda
1 teaspoon ground cinnamon
½ cup canola oil
½ cup sugar
¼ cup brown sugar
1 tablespoon plain soy yogurt
1 teaspoon vanilla extract
1 cup grated carrots
1 cup raisins
½ cup chopped walnuts

SELF-RISING FLOUR

Because it already contains leaveners, self-rising flour is perfect for quick-bread baking. You can also make your own self-rising flour by combining 3 cups flour with 4½ teaspoons baking powder and 1½ teaspoons kosher salt. Blend this mixture well before measuring. Self-rising flour is not a substitute for yeast.

1. Preheat oven to 375°F.

2. In a large bowl, whisk together the flour, salt, baking powder, baking soda, and cinnamon. In a separate bowl, whisk oil, sugar, brown sugar, yogurt, and vanilla until well blended. Add wet ingredients to the flour mixture, stirring until just mixed. Fold in carrots, raisins, and walnuts.

3. Pour batter into greased or paper-lined muffin tins ⅔ full. Bake 20–25 minutes or until a toothpick comes out clean when inserted into the center of the muffins and the tops are golden brown. Allow to cool 15 minutes in pans, then transfer to wire racks.

Peach Muffins

1¾ cups all-purpose flour
1 tablespoon baking powder
¼ teaspoon salt
½ cup sugar
½ cup soymilk
1 teaspoon vanilla extract
2 tablespoons melted vegan margarine
1½ tablespoons apple cider vinegar
1 cup canned drained and diced peaches

1. Preheat oven to 400°F.
2. In a large bowl, whisk together flour, baking powder, salt, and sugar.
   In a separate bowl, combine soymilk, vanilla, melted margarine, and
   vinegar. Quickly combine soymilk mixture with dry ingredients,
   stirring until just mixed. Fold in peaches. Pour batter into greased or
   paper-lined muffin tins ⅔ full.
3. Bake 15–20 minutes or until a toothpick comes out clean when
   inserted into the center of the muffins and the tops are golden brown.

Vegan Pancakes

▶ MAKES 8–10 PANCAKES

1 cup flour
1 tablespoon sugar
1¾ teaspoons baking powder
¼ teaspoon salt
½ banana
1 teaspoon vanilla extract
1 cup soymilk

1. Mix together flour, sugar, baking powder, and salt in a large bowl.

2. In a separate small bowl, mash banana with a fork. Add vanilla and whisk until smooth and fluffy. Add soymilk and stir to combine well.

3. Add soymilk mixture to the flour and dry ingredients, stirring just until combined.

4. Heat a lightly greased griddle or large frying pan over medium heat. Drop batter about 3 tablespoons at a time and heat until bubbles appear on surface, 2–3 minutes. Flip and cook other side until lightly golden brown, another 1–2 minutes.

DON'T OVERMIX!

When it comes to mixing pancake batter, less is more! Pancakes should be light and fluffy, but overmixing the batter will make them tough and rubbery. Gently combine the wet ingredients with the dry ones and don't be afraid of a few lumps; they'll sort themselves out when heated. If you let the batter sit for about five minutes, you'll need to stir even less.

Corny Polenta Breakfast Pancakes

▶ SERVES 8

1 cup coarse yellow cornmeal
2 cups boiling water
1¼ cups flour
1¼ teaspoons table salt
2½ tablespoons sugar
4½ tablespoons baking powder
¾ cup milk
2 large eggs plus 1 large egg white, beaten
5 ounces (1¼ sticks) melted butter
Pure maple syrup for serving

1. Make the polenta by whisking the cornmeal directly into the boiling water. It should quickly thicken to a paste. Transfer immediately to a platter or pan to cool.

2. In a medium bowl, sift together flour, salt, sugar, and baking powder. In a separate bowl, whisk together milk, eggs, and melted butter. Whisk flour mixture into egg mixture, mixing only as much as is necessary to combine. Overmixing will toughen the cakes. Crumble the cooled polenta into the batter, breaking up large pieces between your fingers. Adjust consistency of the batter with additional milk if necessary to achieve the consistency of thick oatmeal.

3. Pour on a hot buttered griddle, cast-iron skillet, or nonstick pan, forming 3"–4" pancakes; cook thoroughly on both sides, 2–3 minutes. Serve with pure maple syrup.

The Quick and Easy Vegetarian College Cookbook

Sweet Potato Apple Latkes

▶ MAKES 12 LATKES

3 large sweet potatoes, peeled and grated
1 medium apple, peeled, cored, and grated
1 small yellow onion, peeled and grated
Egg replacement equal to 2 eggs
3 tablespoons flour
1 teaspoon baking powder
½ teaspoon ground cinnamon
½ teaspoon ground nutmeg
½ teaspoon salt
Oil for frying

1. Using a cloth or paper towel, gently squeeze out excess moisture from grated potatoes and apples; combine with onions in a large bowl.
2. Add remaining ingredients except for oil and mix well.
3. Heat a few tablespoons of oil in a skillet or frying pan. Drop potato mixture in the hot oil a scant ¼ cup at a time and use a spatula to flatten, forming a pancake. Cook 3–4 minutes on each side until lightly crisped.

Tofu Breakfast Burrito

▶ SERVES 2

1 block firm or extra-firm tofu, well
 pressed
2 tablespoons olive oil
½ cup salsa
½ teaspoon chili powder
Salt and freshly ground black pepper to
 taste
2 warmed flour tortillas
Ketchup or hot sauce to taste
2 slices vegan cheese
½ avocado, pitted, peeled, and sliced

SOY CHEESE

Soy cheese is a variety of
cheese analog, which is
a dairy cheese substitute
most commonly made
from soy but also from rice,
almonds, or other nondairy
foods. Many soy cheeses
have calcium added, so that
you still get the benefits of
dairy cheese.

1. Cube or crumble the tofu into 1"
   chunks. Sauté in olive oil in a small skillet over medium heat 2–3
   minutes.

2. Add salsa and chili powder and cook 2–3 more minutes, stirring
   frequently. Season generously with salt and pepper.

3. Layer each warmed flour tortilla with half of the tofu and salsa mix
   and drizzle with ketchup or hot sauce.

4. Add vegan cheese and avocado slices and wrap like a burrito.

Challah French Toast

▶ SERVES 4

½ teaspoon ground cinnamon

3 cups milk

6 extra large eggs, beaten

1 teaspoon vanilla extract

3 tablespoons sugar

1 teaspoon salt

8 (1"-thick) slices challah

2 tablespoons unsalted butter

Pure maple syrup

1. In a mixing bowl, make a paste with the cinnamon and a drop of the milk. Whisk in the rest of the milk, the eggs, vanilla, sugar, and salt. Transfer to a wide, deep dish and submerge the bread slices in the egg mixture. Allow to soak at least 10 minutes, pressing the slices gently under with your fingertips to keep them submerged and turning them halfway through.

2. Heat a large, heavy-bottomed skillet (the best is a cast-iron Griswold) over medium-low heat. A piece of butter should sizzle but not smoke when it is added. Melt ¼ of the butter and fry the soaked bread two pieces at a time (it's important not to crowd the pan) on both sides until they bounce back when poked with a finger, about 4 minutes per side. Serve them as they come out of the pan or keep them warm in the oven. Do not reuse butter—wipe the pan after each batch. Serve with pure maple syrup.

Scones

2 cups cake flour

2 cups all-purpose flour

1½ teaspoons baking powder

1 teaspoon salt

½ cup sugar

4 ounces (1 stick) butter, cut into pieces the size of a hazelnut

4 ounces (1 stick) margarine, cut into pieces the size of a hazelnut

¾ cup currants or raisins (optional)

2 large eggs

About ½ cup milk

1. Preheat oven to 350°F. Whisk together the cake flour, all-purpose flour, baking powder, salt, and sugar in a large bowl until fluffy. Add the butter and margarine; mix with your hands, pinching together the flour between your fingers to coat it. Continue mixing until the flour has taken on the color of the butter and it clumps, but there should still be some nuggets of butter/margarine. Add currants or raisins if using.

2. In a separate small bowl, whisk together the eggs and milk. Add egg mixture to the flour mixture and mix with your hands or a wooden spoon just until combined. Do not overmix, as it will make the batter tough. The consistency should be like oatmeal. Add additional milk if necessary.

3. Drop the batter into 12 scones on an oiled sheet pan. Bake on top shelf of the oven until set, about 20 minutes. For extra color, flash under the broiler for a moment to brown the tops.

APPETIZERS AND SIDES

Artichoke Dip

▶ SERVES 8

2 (15-ounce) cans quartered artichoke hearts, drained and rinsed
1 medium red bell pepper, seeded and finely chopped
1 medium green bell pepper, seeded and finely chopped
3 cloves garlic, peeled and minced
2 cups mayonnaise
Ground white pepper to taste
1 pound grated Parmesan cheese, divided

Preheat oven to 325°F. In a medium bowl, mix all ingredients except ¼ of the Parmesan cheese. Spread into a 9" × 9" baking dish or 1½-quart casserole dish, sprinkle remaining Parmesan over the top, and bake 45 minutes until golden brown. Serve with crackers or bread.

Salsa Fresca (Pico de Gallo)

▶ SERVES 8

1½ cups finely diced tomatoes, divided
1 small white onion, peeled and finely chopped
1 medium jalapeño pepper, seeded and finely chopped
1 tablespoon puréed chipotle in adobo
½ teaspoon salt
2 teaspoons lime juice
¼ cup chopped fresh cilantro

1. In a blender or food processor, purée ⅓ of the tomatoes.
2. In a medium bowl, combine tomato purée with remaining tomatoes, onions, jalapeños, chipotle, salt, lime juice, and cilantro. Best if used within 2 days.

Baba Ghanouj

SERVES 4

2 cloves garlic

1 whole medium eggplant, roasted 1 hour in a 400°F oven, cooled, pulp scooped out

1 tablespoon tahini

1½ teaspoons kosher salt

2–3 teaspoons toasted ground cumin

Juice of 2 medium lemons, divided

¼ cup extra-virgin olive oil plus a little extra for garnish

¼ teaspoon freshly ground black pepper or to taste

Paprika and chopped fresh parsley for garnish

Pita bread for dipping

1. In a food processor or blender, chop the garlic until it sticks to the walls of the processor bowl. Add eggplant pulp, tahini, salt, cumin, and half of the lemon juice. Process until smooth, gradually drizzling in the olive oil. Season to taste with black pepper, additional salt, and lemon juice if necessary.

2. Spread onto plates and garnish with a drizzle of extra-virgin olive oil, a few drops of lemon juice, a dusting of paprika, and some chopped parsley. Serve with wedges of warm pita bread.

Chili-Cheese Dip

▶ SERVES 12

1 (15-ounce) can vegetarian chili
¼ cup diced onions
½ cup diced tomatoes
1 (8-ounce) package cream cheese or
    vegan cream cheese
1 cup Cheddar cheese or vegan Cheddar
1 teaspoon garlic powder

VEGETARIAN CHILI

Most major grocery stores sell canned vegetarian chili. One of the easiest to find is Hormel Chili Vegetarian with Beans, which contains textured vegetable protein instead of meat.

In a 4-quart slow cooker, place all ingredients. Stir gently; cover and heat on low 1 hour.

Red Garlic Mayonnaise (Rouille)

▶ MAKES 1½ CUPS

2 cloves garlic, peeled and chopped very fine
1 cup mayonnaise or soy mayo
1 small roasted red bell pepper, peeled and puréed
Pinch of salt
Juice of ½ medium lemon
Pinch of cayenne pepper

In a medium bowl, whisk together garlic, mayonnaise, and roasted pepper purée. Season with a pinch of salt, a squeeze of lemon, and cayenne.

Spicy White Bean–Citrus Dip

▶ SERVES 12

2 (15-ounce) cans white navy beans,
   drained and rinsed
¼ cup sour cream
1 tablespoon orange juice concentrate
1 teaspoon hot pepper sauce or puréed
   chipotle in adobo
1 teaspoon lime juice
Grated zest of 1 medium orange
½ teaspoon salt
½ cup diced white onions
1 tablespoon chopped cilantro

SMOKY AND SPICY

For a smokier taste, replace the hot pepper sauce with puréed chipotle pepper. Chipotle is a smoked jalapeño pepper. They are sold in small 6-ounce cans and are very useful for imparting a smoky flavor and medium heat to dishes. Purée them with the sauce in which they're packed, using a blender or food processor.

1. Purée the beans, sour cream, orange juice concentrate, hot sauce or chipotle, lime juice, orange zest, and salt in a blender or food processor until smooth. Pour into a medium bowl.

2. Add onions and cilantro; mix with a rubber spatula until combined.

Easy Asian Dipping Sauce

▶ MAKES ⅓ CUP

¼ cup soy sauce
2 tablespoons rice vinegar
2 teaspoons sesame oil
1 teaspoon sugar

1 teaspoon minced fresh ginger
2 cloves garlic, peeled, minced,
   and crushed
¼ teaspoon crushed red pepper or
   to taste

Whisk together all ingredients.

Vegan Spinach and Artichoke Dip

▶ MAKES 4 CUPS

1 (15-ounce) can artichokes,
    drained and chopped
2 cups water
1 teaspoon lemon juice
1 tablespoon vegan margarine
1 cup chopped thawed frozen spinach
8 ounces vegan cream cheese
16 ounces vegan sour cream
⅓ cup vegan Parmesan cheese
¼ teaspoon garlic powder
¼ teaspoon salt

SERVING OPTIONS

This recipe calls for serving the dip warm, but chilling the dip and serving it cool is also delicious. After cooking, let the dip cool to room temperature and store in the refrigerator in an airtight container. Let cool at least 3 hours before serving.

1. In a 4-quart slow cooker, add all ingredients.
2. Cover and cook over low heat 1 hour.

Watercress Dip

▶ MAKES 1½ CUPS

1 bunch watercress, stems trimmed by 1", roughly chopped
1 cup soy mayonnaise
¼ teaspoon salt
¼ teaspoon freshly ground black pepper

In a food processor or blender, purée watercress until very fine, about 1 minute. Add mayonnaise; pulse to combine. Season with salt and pepper.

Hummus

MAKES 2 CUPS

2 cloves garlic

1 (16-ounce) can chickpeas, drained and rinsed

3 tablespoons tahini

½ teaspoon kosher salt

2–3 teaspoons toasted ground cumin

Juice of 1 medium lemon, divided

¼ cup extra-virgin olive oil plus a little extra for garnish

Freshly ground black pepper to taste

Paprika and chopped fresh parsley for garnish (optional)

1. In a food processor or blender, process the garlic until it sticks to the sides of the bowl. Add chickpeas, tahini, salt, cumin, and half of the lemon juice. Process until smooth, gradually drizzling in the olive oil. Add up to ¼ cup cold water to achieve a softer hummus if desired.

2. Season to taste with black pepper and additional salt and lemon juice to taste.

3. Spread onto plates and garnish with a drizzle of extra-virgin olive oil, a few drops of lemon juice, a dusting of paprika, and some chopped parsley.

Guacamole

► SERVES 8

2 cloves garlic, peeled and chopped

¼ cup chopped red onion

1 small jalapeño pepper, seeded and
finely chopped

4 medium ripe Hass avocados, halved,
pitted, and flesh scooped from the
skin

2 tablespoons lime juice

½ teaspoon salt

Freshly ground black pepper to taste

¼ cup chopped cilantro

1 medium plum tomato, seeded and
chopped (optional)

1. In a mortar and pestle, or in a mixing
bowl with a fork, mash together the
garlic, onion, and jalapeño. Add the
avocado and mash until it forms a
chunky paste.

2. Add lime juice, salt, pepper, and
cilantro and stir to combine. Garnish
with chopped tomato if desired.

PITTING AN AVOCADO

Start by cutting through the skin, down to the pit, and scoring the fruit lengthwise. Gripping both halves, give a quick twist to separate one half from the pit, leaving the other half holding the large nut. If you plan to use only half of the avocado, it's best to leave the pit in the unused portion, since it prevents the fruit from turning brown overnight. To remove the pit, hack into the middle of it with the blade of your knife, gripping the fruit in the palm of your other hand; twist the knife clockwise to loosen the pit. It should fall right out of a ripe avocado.

Mango Citrus Salsa

MAKES 2 CUPS

1 medium mango, peeled, pitted, and chopped

2 medium tangerines, peeled and chopped

½ medium red bell pepper, seeded and chopped

½ medium red onion, peeled and minced

3 cloves garlic, peeled and minced

½ medium jalapeño pepper, seeded and minced

2 tablespoons lime juice

½ teaspoon salt

¼ teaspoon freshly ground black pepper

3 tablespoons chopped fresh cilantro

HELLO, MANGO!

A ripe mango is sweet with a unique taste that varies from variety to variety. The texture of the flesh varies as well, some having a soft, pulpy texture similar to an overripe plum, while others have firmer flesh like a cantaloupe or avocado. Mango lassi, or a mango smoothie, is a very popular choice in many Indian restaurants.

1. Gently toss together all ingredients in a large bowl.

2. Allow to sit at least 15 minutes before serving to allow flavors to mingle.

Tapenade

MAKES 1 CUP

½ cup green olives

¾ cup black olives

2 cloves garlic

1 tablespoon capers (optional)

2 tablespoons lemon juice

2 tablespoons olive oil

¼ teaspoon oregano

¼ teaspoon black pepper

Process all ingredients in a blender or food processor until almost smooth.

Rancheros Salsa

2 tablespoons olive oil
1 medium white onion, peeled and roughly chopped
1 medium red bell pepper, seeded and roughly chopped
1 medium green bell pepper, seeded and roughly chopped
4 medium plum tomatoes, seeded and roughly chopped
1 tablespoon chopped garlic (about 4 cloves)
1 (14-ounce) can diced tomatoes in tomato purée
1 (7-ounce) can tomatillos, drained
1 (7-ounce) can green chilies, rinsed, drained, and roughly chopped
1 teaspoon chipotle purée (optional)
1 medium jalapeño pepper, seeded and finely chopped
¼ cup chopped fresh cilantro
1 tablespoon frozen orange juice concentrate
1 teaspoon ground cumin, toasted in a dry pan until fragrant
1 teaspoon dried oregano
¼ teaspoon ground cinnamon
Salt and freshly ground black pepper to taste

In a large heavy-bottomed pot, heat the oil over medium-high heat until hot but not smoky. Add onion, peppers, and plum tomatoes; cook 5 minutes until onion is translucent. In a food processor or blender, purée garlic, diced tomato, and tomatillos; add to onion mixture. Cook 5 minutes more. Add chilies, chipotle, jalapeño, and cilantro; stir in orange juice concentrate, cumin, oregano, cinnamon, salt, and pepper. Cook 5 minutes more.

Fresh Basil Bruschetta with Balsamic Reduction

▶ SERVES 4

¾ cup balsamic vinegar

1 tablespoon sugar

2 large tomatoes, diced small

3 cloves garlic, peeled and minced

¼ cup chopped fresh basil

2 tablespoons olive oil

Salt and freshly ground black pepper to taste

8–10 slices French bread

A TUSCAN TRADITION

A true Italian chef will prepare the bread for bruschetta by toasting homemade bread over hot coals, then quickly rubbing a sliced clove of garlic over both sides of the bread before drizzling with just a touch of the finest olive oil. In lieu of hot coals, a toaster or 5 minutes in the oven at 350°F will work just fine.

1. Whisk together the balsamic vinegar and sugar in a small saucepan. Bring to a boil, then reduce to a slow simmer. Allow to cook 6–8 minutes until almost thickened. Remove from heat.

2. Combine the tomatoes, garlic, basil, olive oil, salt, and pepper in a large bowl. Gently toss with balsamic sauce.

3. Spoon tomato mixture over bread slices and serve immediately.

Fried Green Tomato "Bruschetta"

4 medium green tomatoes, sliced ½" thick

Flour, eggs, and bread crumbs for dredging

Oil for frying (preferably olive oil)

1 tablespoon balsamic vinegar

¼ cup chopped fresh basil leaves (plus a few whole leaves for garnish)

12 green olives with pimento, halved lengthwise

¼ cup extra-virgin olive oil

1 loaf crusty country bread, sliced 1" thick

1. Dredge tomato slices in flour, eggs, and bread crumbs, shaking off excess after each dip, and fry them at low heat (about 325°F) until golden and mostly tender (a little underdone is good). Place the still-hot tomatoes flat on a cutting board and dice them into ½" pieces.

2. In a large mixing bowl, gently toss the diced tomatoes with the vinegar, basil, and olives. Set aside.

3. Brush the bread slices with extra-virgin oil and grill or oven-toast (400°F) until lightly browned. This can also be done under the broiler. Top each of 6 slices with tomato mixture, cut each in half, and serve garnished with a small basil sprig.

Tomato and Black Olive Bruschetta

▶ SERVES 8

4 slices Italian country bread or other crusty rustic bread, about ½" thick
½ cup extra-virgin olive oil
2 cloves garlic, peeled and finely chopped
3 medium ripe tomatoes, roughly chopped
½ teaspoon salt
¼ teaspoon freshly ground black pepper
½ cup Gaeta, kalamata, or oil-cured black olives (about 24), pitted
¼ cup roughly chopped fresh Italian parsley
Juice of 1 medium lemon

1. Heat a stovetop grill, barbecue grill, or broiler. Cut the bread slices in half.

2. In a small bowl, combine the olive oil and garlic; brush the bread liberally with some of this garlic oil using a pastry brush or your hands. Grill or broil until well toasted on both sides.

3. In a medium bowl, toss chopped tomatoes with 1 tablespoon garlic oil (make sure to get some pieces of garlic in there), salt, pepper, olives, and parsley. Season to taste with lemon juice.

4. Top each piece of grilled bread with a small mound of tomato-olive mixture. Arrange neatly on a serving platter.

Country Corn Cakes

▶ SERVES 4

1 cup buttermilk

1 large egg, lightly beaten

2 tablespoons melted butter

1 cup uncooked grits or coarse cornmeal

1 cup all-purpose flour

1 cup corn kernels, preferably fresh

1 cup cooked black-eyed peas

1 tablespoon baking powder

1 teaspoon baking soda

Salt and freshly ground black pepper to taste

Vegetable oil for pan-frying

ABOUT BLACK-EYED PEAS

If you live in the South, you know the tradition: eat black-eyed peas on New Year's Day to bring good luck for the rest of the year. But these delicious legumes, also known as "cow peas," should be enjoyed often. These "peas" (they are actually beans) are rich sources of calcium, potassium, protein, and vitamin A.

1. Combine the buttermilk, egg, and butter in a large mixing bowl. Stir in the grits, flour, corn kernels, black-eyed peas, baking powder, baking soda, salt, and pepper; the batter will be thick.

2. Heat about 2 tablespoons vegetable oil in a large skillet or on a griddle over medium to medium-low heat. When the surface is hot, spoon about ¾ cup batter per cake onto the surface, and when the bottom has browned, carefully turn the cake over to cook the second side. Be sure the skillet does not overheat or the cakes will burn. Repeat until all the batter is used up, adding more oil as needed. Serve hot.

Crudités with Three Dips

▶ SERVES 8

6 cups assorted vegetables (such as carrot sticks, celery sticks, various colored bell peppers, zucchini and yellow squash, radishes, blanched broccoli florets, cauliflower florets and green beans, fennel, cooked beets), cut into bite-sized pieces

Assorted black and green olives

Rosemary or thyme sprigs for garnish

3 dressings or dips, such as Spicy White Bean–Citrus Dip, Vegan Spinach and Artichoke Dip, and Hummus (see recipes in this chapter)

Arrange vegetables attractively on a serving platter or in a basket, placing different colors beside one another. Garnish with olives and herb sprigs. Serve with dips or drizzled with any dressing.

Spiced Pecans

▶ MAKES 3 CUPS

1 ounce (2 tablespoons) unsalted butter

1 pound whole, shelled pecans

2 tablespoons light soy sauce

1 tablespoon hoisin sauce

1–2 drops hot pepper sauce

1. Preheat oven to 325°F.
2. Melt butter in a large skillet. Add nuts and cook, tossing occasionally until nuts are well coated. Add soy sauce, hoisin sauce, and hot pepper sauce; cook 1 minute more. Stir to coat thoroughly.
3. Spread nuts in a single layer on a baking sheet. Bake until all liquid is absorbed and nuts begin to brown. Remove from oven. Cool before serving.

Eggplant Caviar

> SERVES 4

1 large eggplant
2 tablespoons olive oil
1 large onion, peeled and finely chopped
3 cloves garlic, peeled and finely chopped
1 tablespoon tomato paste
Salt and freshly ground black pepper to taste
Crackers or French bread

1. Preheat oven to 400°F. Place eggplant in a baking dish and roast on middle rack of the oven until very well done, about 1 hour; cool. Cut the eggplant in half and scoop out the soft pulp with a serving spoon. Place on a cutting board and chop thoroughly until it has the consistency of oatmeal.

2. Heat the olive oil in a large skillet over medium heat for 1 minute. Add onions; cook until very soft but not brown, about 10 minutes; add garlic and cook 1 minute more. Stir in tomato paste; cook 1 minute.

3. Add chopped eggplant and cook until mixture is thickened. An indentation should remain when a spoon is depressed into the mixture. Season with salt and pepper to taste. Serve with crackers or sliced French bread.

Fresh Mint Spring Rolls

▶ SERVES 3 OR 4

1 (3-ounce) package clear bean thread
   noodles
1 cup hot water
1 tablespoon soy sauce
½ teaspoon ground ginger
1 teaspoon sesame oil
¼ cup diced shiitake mushrooms
1 medium carrot, peeled and grated
10–12 spring roll wrappers
Warm water
½ head green leaf lettuce, chopped
1 cucumber, peeled and sliced thin
1 bunch fresh mint

TO DIP OR NOT TO DIP?

Store-bought sweet chili sauce, spicy sriracha sauce, or a Japanese salad dressing or marinade will work in a pinch, but a simple homemade dip is best for these spring rolls. Try the Easy Asian Dipping Sauce (see recipe in this chapter).

1. Break noodles in half to make smaller pieces, then submerge in 1 cup hot water until soft, 6–7 minutes. Drain.

2. In a large bowl, toss together the hot noodles with the soy sauce, ginger, sesame oil, mushrooms, and carrots, tossing well to combine.

3. In a large shallow pan, carefully submerge spring roll wrappers one at a time in warm water until just barely soft. Remove from water and place a bit of lettuce in the center of the wrapper. Add about 2 tablespoons of noodles mixture, a few slices of cucumber, and place 2–3 mint leaves on top.

4. Fold the bottom of the wrapper over the filling, fold in each sides, then roll.

Ginger-Vegetable Spring Rolls

▶ SERVES 12

1 cup shredded red cabbage
½ cup shredded carrot
½ cup chopped green onion
½ cup chopped celery
½ cup diced extra-firm tofu
1 tablespoon grated fresh ginger
2 teaspoons minced garlic
2 tablespoons sesame oil
2 tablespoons soy sauce
12 vegan spring roll wrappers
2 tablespoons water
1 tablespoon vegetable oil

1. Preheat oven to 425°F and prepare an oven grate with olive oil spray.

2. In a large mixing bowl, combine the cabbage, carrots, onion, celery, tofu, ginger, and garlic. Add the sesame oil and soy sauce to the mixture and blend well until ingredients are combined thoroughly and wet.

3. In the center of each spring roll wrapper, place 2 tablespoons vegetable mixture. Fold wrappers as when wrapping enchiladas: wet the edges of the wrapper, fold in the right and left sides to cover edges of mixture, and roll to enclose completely.

4. Lay the spring rolls on the prepared grate; use fingers or a pastry brush to lightly coat the spring rolls with the vegetable oil.

5. Bake 15 minutes, turn, and continue baking an additional 5–10 minutes or until spring rolls are brown and crispy.

VEGAN PRODUCTS NOW WIDELY AVAILABLE

You may be surprised to see that there are now vegan spring roll wrappers available, but it's true! Because the vegan lifestyle has become so popular throughout the world, many manufacturers have decided to dip into the ever-growing industry of healthy vegan alternatives by providing their own products and adhering to vegan standards! The next time you think you have to skip a recipe just because it has an ingredient that you doubt is offered vegan-style, check your local grocer or health food store and you may be pleasantly surprised!

Manchego-Potato Tacos with Pickled Jalapeños

▶ SERVES 8

1 cup leftover mashed potatoes

8 soft corn tortillas

¼ pound manchego cheese or sharp Cheddar, cut into 16 small sticks

16 slices pickled jalapeño pepper

4 tablespoons unsalted butter

1. Spoon 1 tablespoon mashed potato into the center of each tortilla. Flatten out the potatoes, leaving a 1" border. Lay 2 pieces of cheese and 2 pieces of jalapeño onto each tortilla and fold closed into a half-moon shape.

2. In a skillet over medium heat, melt half of the butter. Gently lay 4 of the tacos into the pan and cook until nicely browned, 3–4 minutes on each side. Drain on paper towels. Repeat with remaining tacos. Snip tacos in half before serving.

SOFTENING STORE-BOUGHT TORTILLAS

Right from the package, corn tortillas are cardboardy and mealy, and flour tortillas are tough like leather. Both should be exposed to either dry or moist heat for 1 minute before serving. This is done either by steaming them for 1 minute, one at a time, in a standard steamer basket, or by placing them directly onto the burner of a gas stove, allowing the flames to lightly brown the tortillas on both sides. You'll notice a definite "puff" in most tortillas when properly softened. Another alternative is to toast briefly in a toaster oven.

Mini Lentil-Scallion Pancakes with Cumin Cream

▶ SERVES 8

1 cup brown lentils, boiled until soft but not broken

3 scallions, chopped fine

1 tablespoon curry powder, toasted in a dry pan until fragrant

Pinch of cayenne pepper

1 teaspoon salt

¼ cup chopped fresh cilantro or parsley

1 egg, beaten

1 tablespoon milk or water

1 tablespoon all-purpose flour

3 tablespoons olive oil for frying

1 cup sour cream

2 teaspoons cumin seeds, toasted in a dry pan then ground (or 2 teaspoons ground cumin toasted in a dry pan until fragrant)

1. Gently combine lentils, scallions, curry, cayenne, salt, and cilantro (or parsley) in a medium mixing bowl. Mix in the beaten egg and milk (or water) with your hands and dust with enough flour to form a cohesive batter.

2. Heat oil in a large nonstick skillet until hot but not smoky. A bit of the batter should sizzle when placed in the oil. Drop teaspoonfuls of batter into the pan; flatten them out and shape them into round cakes with the back of the spoon. Some lentils may fall away, but the cakes will stick together once they're cooked. Leave at least 1" of space between cakes. Fry 2–3 minutes per side until lightly browned and crisp. Drain on paper towels.

3. In a small bowl, whisk together the sour cream and cumin. Arrange the lentil cakes on a serving platter and top each with a dollop of cumin cream.

Potato Pakoras (Fritters)

▶ SERVES 8

1¼ cups sifted chickpea flour

2 teaspoons vegetable oil

1½ teaspoons ground cumin

½ teaspoon cayenne pepper or paprika

¼ teaspoon ground turmeric

2½ teaspoons salt

Approximately ½ cup cold water

1 large or 2 medium baking potatoes (about 8 ounces), peeled, then sliced into ⅛" pieces

Oil for frying

1. In a food processor or blender, pulse flour, oil, cumin, cayenne, turmeric, and salt 3 or 4 times until fluffy. With blade spinning, gradually add water and process 2–3 minutes until smooth. Adjust consistency by adding water until the mixture is slightly thicker than the consistency of heavy cream. Cover and set aside 10 minutes.

2. Heat fry oil to 350°F. Dip potato slices into batter one by one, then slip them into the fry oil in batches of 6 or 7. Fry 4–5 minutes each side until golden brown and cooked through. Serve immediately with chutney for dipping.

Mini Goat Cheese Pizzas

▶ SERVES 8

1 (17-ounce) package frozen puff pastry
　　dough, thawed
3 medium Roma tomatoes, thinly sliced
1 (4-ounce) package fresh goat cheese
2 tablespoons chopped fresh thyme or
　　parsley

1. Preheat oven to 400°F.

2. Spread pastry on a lightly floured
surface and cut out 8 (4") disks. Place
disks on a large ungreased baking
sheet. Stack another, matching pan
atop the disks and bake until golden
brown, about 15 minutes. The second
pan will keep the disks from rising
too high.

3. Top each disk with 2 or 3 slices
tomato, ½ ounce goat cheese, and
about ½ teaspoon chopped thyme.
To serve, warm again in the oven 1
minute until the goat cheese attains a
slight shimmer; serve hot.

CRUMBLING GOAT CHEESE

Cold from the refrigerator, goat cheese crumbles between the fingers, or by flaking it away with the tines of a fork, into attractive snowy-white nuggets. Chèvre is usually sold in 3- to 4-ounce logs. Push the tines of a fork down into the open end of a log and pry down, twisting to produce attractive crumbs perfect for sprinkling on salads, garnishing soups, or piling on small rounds of French bread.

Sweet Potato and Rosemary Pizza

► SERVES 6

1 can store-bought pizza crust or pizza
   dough of your choice

1½ tablespoons extra-virgin olive oil

1 large sweet potato, peeled

2 sprigs fresh rosemary or 1 teaspoon
   dried rosemary leaves

Salt and freshly ground black pepper to
   taste

**WHAT IS A DOUBLED-
UP SHEET PAN?**

To buffer baking foods
from the direct heat of oven
elements, chefs often stack
two identical baking sheets
(known in the industry as
"sheet pans") together,
creating an air pocket
that protects food from
burning on the bottom.
Commercially manufactured
pans, such as Bakers'
Secret pans, incorporate
this concept into their
insulated bakeware.

1. Preheat oven to 400°F. Spread dough to ¼" thickness onto a doubled-up, lightly greased sheet pan. Brush on a light coating of olive oil.

2. Shred the sweet potato into a ¼"-thick layer over the pizza crust using the large-holed side of a box grater. Distribute rosemary leaves evenly on top of potato. Sprinkle remaining olive oil over the pizza and season it with salt and pepper.

3. Bake 20–25 minutes until potato is cooked through and begins to brown.

Spicy Jalapeño Poppers

▶ SERVES 12

1 cup low-fat plain Greek-style yogurt or vegan yogurt
½ medium red onion, peeled and minced
½ cup minced tomatoes
2 tablespoons minced garlic
1 teaspoon all-natural sea salt
12 medium jalapeño peppers
1 cup almond milk
1 cup 100% whole-wheat flour
½ cup olive oil

1. In a medium mixing bowl, combine yogurt, onion, tomatoes, garlic, and salt.

2. Remove tops and seeds from jalapeños, then stuff with the yogurt mixture.

3. Pour almond milk into a shallow dish next to a shallow dish filled with the whole-wheat flour.

4. Dip each jalapeño into the almond milk and roll in the flour; set aside.

5. Heat the olive oil in a large skillet over medium heat. Add the jalapeños and cook until golden brown all over, turning regularly.

6. Remove from oil and place onto paper towels to soak up excess oil.

Stuffed Mushrooms

▶ SERVES 6

1 pound mushrooms (caps approximately 1½" across)
3 tablespoons butter
½ cup finely chopped onion
¾ cup bread crumbs
½ teaspoon salt
Freshly ground black pepper to taste
1 teaspoon dried thyme
¼ cup half-and-half
¼ cup grated Parmesan cheese
2 tablespoons chopped fresh parsley

1. Preheat oven broiler. Clean the mushrooms and gently pull the stem from each cap, setting the caps aside. Chop the mushroom stems and set aside. Heat butter in a medium skillet over medium heat. Add onion and cook 2 minutes until translucent. Add mushroom stems and cook 2–3 minutes more. Stir in bread crumbs, salt, pepper, and thyme; cook 1 minute more. Remove from heat and stir in half-and-half and grated cheese.

2. Using a small spoon, fill each mushroom cap with the mushroom mixture. Place the filled mushrooms on a baking sheet and put under the preheated oven broiler 5–7 minutes until the tops are browned and the caps have softened and become juicy. Sprinkle the tops with chopped parsley and serve hot or warm.

Stuffed Pepper Poppers

► SERVES 16

20 mini bell peppers of assorted colors
1 cup cooked brown rice
1 cup Salsa Fresca (see recipe in this
   chapter)
1 cup kernel corn (fresh or thawed from
   frozen)
1 cup cooked black beans
1 teaspoon ground cumin
1 cup chopped romaine lettuce

1. To prepare peppers, remove tops
   and scoop out ribs and seeds. Set
   16 aside and chop 4 to use in
   stuffing mixture.

2. In a large mixing bowl, combine the
   chopped bell peppers, cooked rice,
   salsa, corn, beans, and cumin. Mix
   ingredients until well blended. Add
   romaine to the mixture and blend by
   tossing gently.

3. Set the mini peppers with the tops
   open-side up. Pack filling into each of
   the peppers up to the top. Press gently to compact.

AMAZING APPS THAT GO ABOVE AND BEYOND DELICIOUSNESS

When it comes to great appetizers in a clean diet, foods that can deliver lots of great taste and lots of great nutrition are top-notch meal starters. Even better, if those healthy apps can provide a combination of complex carbohydrates, clean protein, and fats that provides a feeling of fullness that lasts and lasts, you've got an extraordinary appetizer that goes above and beyond the everyday variety.

Sweet Fennel with Lemon and Shaved Parmigiano-Reggiano

▶ SERVES 4

2 bulbs fresh fennel

½ fresh lemon

1 wedge (at least 4" long) Parmigiano-Reggiano or Asiago cheese

1 tablespoon very high quality extra-virgin olive oil

Pinch of salt

1. Trim the stems and fronds from the fennel tops. Break the bulbs apart layer by layer using your hands to make long, bite-sized pieces. Discard the core. Arrange the pieces in a pyramid shape onto a small, attractive serving plate.

2. Squeeze the lemon over the fennel. Using a peeler, shave curls of cheese over the fennel, allowing them to fall where they may; make about 10 curls.

3. Drizzle the olive oil over the plate and sprinkle with salt. Serve at room temperature.

EVEN-SEASONING SECRET

To avoid salty patches in some parts of your food and bland, unseasoned patches on other parts, take a cue from pro chefs: season from a great height. Most chefs pinch salt between their thumb and forefinger and sprinkle it down onto food from a great height, more than a foot above the item being seasoned. It tends to shower broadly over the food this way, covering evenly.

Veggie-Packed Potato Skins

▶ SERVES 12

6 baked Idaho potatoes

1 tablespoon extra-virgin olive oil

1 cup chopped red onion

1 cup chopped zucchini

1 cup sliced mushrooms

2 tablespoons water

1 teaspoon all-natural sea salt, divided

1 teaspoon freshly ground black pepper, divided

1 teaspoon garlic powder, divided

1 teaspoon ground cumin, divided

1 cup nonfat Greek-style yogurt or soy yogurt

2–3 medium Roma tomatoes, chopped

1. Allow potatoes to cool after baking, cut in half lengthwise, and scoop out the inside of the potatoes leaving ⅛"–¼" of flesh. Save 1 cup of scooped potatoes for stuffing mixture.

2. In a large skillet over medium heat, heat the olive oil until runny and smooth. Sauté the red onion about 2 minutes or until slightly tender. Add the zucchini, mushrooms, and 2 tablespoons water to the onions. Sprinkle with ½ teaspoon each of the salt, pepper, garlic powder, and cumin; sauté 5–6 minutes or until fork-tender.

MAKE THE HEALTHY SWITCH HERE . . . AND THERE

Many people dread the word "diet" because the stigma of dieting is wound tightly around deprivation and starvation. One of the greatest aspects of clean eating is that you can enjoy the foods you love; you just need to be creative and find ways to use natural, whole ingredients more often. Classic restaurant favorites like potato skins come packed with unhealthy ingredients and are topped with even more of the same; you can enjoy a healthier version of the same food that packs flavor, texture, and tons of nutrition . . . without the guilt and bloat of the restaurant-made alternative.

3. Move the sautéed vegetables to the mixing bowl and combine thoroughly with the potatoes. Add the yogurt and remaining salt, pepper, garlic powder, and cumin; mix together until chunky and combined well.

4. Spoon the mixture into the potato skins and pack by pressing firmly. Garnish with chopped tomatoes.

Wild Mushroom Ragout in Puff Pastry Shells

▶ SERVES 8

24 pieces frozen puff pastry hors d'oeuvre shells
1 tablespoon unsalted butter
2 cups (about ½ pound) assorted wild mushrooms, such as morels, chanterelles, oysters, shiitakes, and/or domestic and cremini mushrooms
½ teaspoon salt, divided
2 sprigs fresh rosemary, leaves picked and chopped
¼ cup Vegetable Stock (see recipe in Chapter 5) or water
1 teaspoon cornstarch dissolved in 1 tablespoon cold water
Freshly ground black pepper to taste
Squeeze of lemon

1. Bake puff pastry shells according to package directions. In a medium skillet over medium heat, melt the butter. Add the mushrooms and cook without stirring 5 minutes until a nice brown coating has developed. Add salt and rosemary; cook 3 minutes more. Add the stock and cornstarch; stir until thickened and bubbling. Remove from heat; adjust seasoning with black pepper, a few drops of lemon juice, and remaining salt to taste.

2. Spoon ½ teaspoon of mushroom ragout into each shell. Serve piping hot.

Vegetable Gado-Gado

16 each: 2" carrot sticks, broccoli florets, trimmed green beans, batons of
  yellow bell pepper and/or yellow summer squash, and assorted other
  vegetables
½ cup smooth peanut butter
¼ cup honey
¼ teaspoon salt
⅛ teaspoon cayenne pepper
1 tablespoon lime juice
¾ cup (6 ounces) coconut milk

1. Blanch all the vegetables quickly in a large pot of lightly salted boiling
   water; plunge immediately into a large bowl of ice-cold water to stop
   the cooking process. Drain and arrange in an attractive pattern on a
   serving platter.

2. Combine peanut butter, honey, salt, cayenne, and lemon juice in a
   food processor or mixing bowl; pulse or whisk together until smooth.
   Gradually work in coconut milk until a saucy consistency is reached.
   Adjust consistency further if desired with hot water. Serve sauce
   alongside blanched vegetables.

SALADS AND DRESSINGS

Cucumber Tabbouleh Salad

▶ SERVES 2

2 large cucumbers, peeled and chopped
2 tablespoons extra-virgin olive oil
2 tablespoons red wine vinegar
2 cups cooked bulgur

1. Combine the cucumbers, olive oil, and vinegar in a mixing bowl and toss to combine.
2. Fold the bulgur into the cucumber mix and combine thoroughly.
3. Refrigerate 1 hour and serve in two salad bowls.

CUCUMBERS FOR . . . EVERYTHING

Not only are cucumbers heralded for their high water content, they are also packed with an amazing nutrient called silica, which may make your skin look and feel younger, your nails stronger, and your hair shinier. Cucumbers also produce lignans, which scientists believe might have a role in preventing certain estrogen-related cancers.

Ginger-Citrus-Apple Salad

▶ SERVES 2

1 medium red grapefruit, peeled and
   seeded
2 medium oranges, peeled and seeded
1 pineapple, peeled and cored
2 medium Granny Smith apples, cored
3 tablespoons lemon juice
2 tablespoons grated fresh ginger

1. Cut the grapefruit, oranges,
   pineapple, and apples into bite-sized
   pieces. Place all fruit in a shallow
   glass bowl.
2. Sprinkle the fruit with the lemon
   juice and top with the grated ginger.
   Toss to coat evenly. Cover and
   marinate for 1 hour before serving,
   tossing every 15–20 minutes to
   prevent the apple from discoloring.

APPLES FOR FULLNESS

Studies have shown that when a person consumes an apple in its natural state, as opposed to its mashed or juiced variations, participants reported feeling full and satisfied for longer periods of time. The natural whole fruit offers up soluble and insoluble fiber that aids in the body's processes of flushing out waste, while providing a feeling of fullness that lasts due to the more extensive digestion required to move the fiber through.

Crisp Romaine Salad with Balsamic Tomatoes

▶ SERVES 2

1 teaspoon maple syrup
1 cup balsamic vinegar
2 pints grape tomatoes
2 large heads romaine lettuce

1. In a mixing bowl, combine the maple syrup and balsamic vinegar. Prick grape tomatoes with a fork and toss in the balsamic mixture. Cover and marinate for one hour.

2. Remove the hard "spine" of the romaine leaves and discard. Rip or chop the leaves and combine with the balsamic tomatoes tossing to coat thoroughly.

3. Serve cold.

GET YOUR DAILY DOSE OF VITAMINS FROM A BOWL OF ROMAINE

If you're looking to satisfy your taste for refreshing crunch and your body's needs for essential vitamins, look no further than a healthy head of romaine lettuce. Packing an astounding amount of vitamins A, K, and C, romaine lettuce is an all-in-one-bowl diet delight of quality nutrition and taste. Providing more than 150 percent of vitamin A, 120 percent of vitamin K, and more than a third of your daily need of vitamin C, romaine lettuce is a refreshing, tasty, and satisfying way to eat up nutrition in versatile style.

Antipasto Salad

▶ SERVES 4

2 cups pitted black olives
2 cups artichoke hearts
2 cups roasted red pepper strips
8 pepperoncini peppers
1 cup sliced banana peppers
4 tablespoons white vinegar
4 cups chopped romaine
2 tablespoons red wine vinegar
2 tablespoons olive oil
1 tablespoon dried oregano

AVOID SODIUM SWELLING

By eliminating foods that are packed with sodium, you can beat the bloat. By creating delicious dishes with natural, whole foods that contain naturally low levels of sodium and provide other essential minerals that aid in normalizing the body's fluids, you can enjoy your favorite dishes without the swelling and heaviness that can result from sodium-packed meals and snacks.

1. In a large shallow dish, combine the olives, artichokes, red peppers, pepperoncini and banana peppers, and white vinegar. Soak 1 hour, tossing occasionally.

2. In a large mixing bowl, combine the romaine, red wine vinegar, olive oil, and oregano and toss to coat.

3. Drain the vegetables and add them to the romaine. Toss to blend thoroughly.

Colorful Vegetable-Pasta Salad

▶ SERVES 2

1 large yellow pepper, seeded and
   sliced
1 large red pepper, seeded and sliced
1 cup sliced yellow onion
1 cup sliced zucchini
1 tablespoon olive oil
1 teaspoon all-natural sea salt
2 cups cooked 100% whole-wheat
   rigatoni
2 tablespoons balsamic vinegar

**BELL PEPPERS FOR
BETTER HEALTH**

With almost 300 percent
of the daily recommended
value of vitamin C, yellow
and orange peppers can
lend health benefits and a
delightfully fruity taste to
any dish.

1. In a large skillet over medium heat, sauté the sliced vegetables with
   the olive oil and sea salt until tender, about 5 minutes.

2. Remove the vegetables from the heat and allow to cool.

3. In a large mixing bowl, combine the sautéed vegetables, cooked
   pasta, and balsamic until thoroughly combined.

Cucumber-Melon Salad

► SERVES 2

2 large cucumbers, peeled
½ medium cantaloupe, peeled and
   seeded
½ medium honeydew, peeled and
   seeded

2 cups watermelon chunks
1 tablespoon agave nectar
1 tablespoon lemon juice

1. Slice cucumbers lengthwise and then into ¼"-thick pieces. Either use a melon baller to form melons into bite-sized balls or cut the cantaloupe and honeydew into bite-sized chunks; cut the watermelon into same size pieces.

2. In a small mixing bowl, whisk together the agave and lemon juice until thoroughly combined.

3. Add the melon pieces to the mixing bowl and toss to coat completely. Serve immediately or cover and marinate 1 hour, tossing every 15–20 minutes.

Lighter Waldorf Salad

► SERVES 2

2 cups shredded romaine lettuce
½ medium Granny Smith apple,
   cored and chopped
1 celery stalk, chopped
½ cup halved red grapes

¼ cup nonfat Greek-style or soy
   yogurt
1 tablespoon maple syrup
1 teaspoon ground nutmeg
½ cup crushed walnuts

1. In a large salad bowl, combine the romaine, apple, celery, and grapes and toss to combine.

2. In a small bowl, combine the yogurt, maple syrup, and nutmeg and blend well.

3. Plate equal amounts of the salad into two salad bowls, top with equal amounts of the sweetened yogurt mixture, and sprinkle with crushed walnuts.

Avocados and Greens

► SERVES 2

2 limes, juiced (about ½ cup)

1 tablespoon agave nectar

3 tablespoons red wine vinegar

1 teaspoon all-natural sea salt

1 large Hass avocado, peeled, pitted, and flesh sliced into ¼"-thick lengthwise strips

¼ pound cherry tomatoes, halved

½ pound baby spinach leaves, washed

1. In a mixing bowl, combine the lime juice, agave nectar, red wine vinegar, and salt. Whisk well until combined.

2. Add the avocados and halved cherry tomatoes to the lime juice and agave mixture. Toss to coat, cover, and refrigerate for 20 minutes.

3. Add baby spinach to the marinated avocados and tomatoes; toss to combine thoroughly. Serve immediately.

AVOCADOS AID IN CAROTENOID ABSORPTION

The next time you sit down to enjoy a meal that includes vibrant carotenoid-packed vegetables like carrots, spinach, and peppers, adding avocado to your plate can help your body absorb those essential anti-inflammatory antioxidants by a whopping 200–400 percent! Because of the healthy fat content in avocados, consuming them at the same time as fat-soluble foods helps your body absorb more of the carotenoid content in the foods rather than passing it up as it passes through.

Citrus, Fennel, and Spinach Salad

▶ SERVES 2

1 tablespoon extra-virgin olive oil

1 lemon, juiced (about ¼ cup)

1 tablespoon agave nectar

1 medium red grapefruit, peeled and seeded, and cut into bite-sized chunks

1 medium white grapefruit, peeled and seeded, and cut into bite-sized chunks

2 medium oranges, peeled and seeded, and cut into bite-sized chunks

1 fennel bulb, cut into bite-sized chunks

2 cups baby spinach, washed

1. In a mixing bowl, combine the olive oil, lemon juice, and agave and whisk to combine thoroughly.

2. Add the grapefruits, oranges, and fennel to the mixing bowl with the olive oil, lemon juice, and agave; toss to coat.

3. Add the spinach and toss to coat. Serve immediately or cover and refrigerate 1 hour before serving.

Spicy Cilantro-Tomato Salad

▶ SERVES 2

½ cup chopped cilantro

¼ cup extra-virgin olive oil

¼ cup balsamic vinegar

2 large tomatoes, cored and quartered

1 cup romaine hearts, rinsed and torn
   into bite-sized pieces

1 cup spicy arugula, rinsed

1 teaspoon all-natural sea salt

1 teaspoon freshly ground black pepper

½ cup crumbled goat cheese

1. In a large salad bowl, combine the cilantro, olive oil, and balsamic vinegar and whisk until well blended. Add the tomatoes to the cilantro mixture, cover, and marinate 1 hour.

2. Toss the romaine heart pieces and arugula in the marinated tomatoes mixture, sprinkle with sea salt and pepper, and plate equal amounts on two salad plates.

3. Top with goat cheese and serve.

ILLNESS PREVENTION FROM SPICY CILANTRO

While this spice may be one of your favorites because of its delicious taste and unique flavor, you'll be happy to know that on top of its powerful aromatic essence, cilantro is a spice that protects the body's cells from free-radical damage. Studies have shown that cilantro actually acts to protect the cells from mutations, and acts as an antimicrobial to prevent certain types of bacteria from invading the body's delicate systems.

Strawberry-Walnut-Flaxseed Salad

▶ SERVES 2

4 cups strawberries, tops removed and
    quartered
1 cup crushed walnuts
2 tablespoons ground flaxseed
1 tablespoon red wine vinegar
½ tablespoon agave nectar
2 sprigs mint leaves

1. Add the strawberries, walnuts, and ground flaxseed to a mixing bowl.

2. Drizzle the red wine vinegar and agave over the salad and toss to coat.

3. Split the salad between two salad bowls, garnish each with a mint sprig, and serve.

> **SNEAK EXTRA NUTRITION INTO EVERY BITE**
>
> Adding a beautiful appearance, a nutty flavor, and a delicious crunch to your salads, flaxseed also contributes essential fats to your favorite foods. You can top salads, pastas, entrées, and even sandwiches with these delightful golden seeds of deliciously nutty-tasting nutrition and relish the flavor and benefits!

Asian Almond-Mandarin Salad

▶ SERVES 2

1 tablespoon rice wine vinegar
1 tablespoon sesame oil
1 teaspoon agave nectar
1 tablespoon minced fresh ginger

2 cups chopped endive leaves
½ cup slivered almonds
1 cup mandarin oranges slices

1. In a mixing bowl, whisk together the vinegar, sesame oil, agave, and minced ginger until well blended.

2. Toss the chopped endive leaves in the dressing to coat.

3. Split the salad between two salad bowls.

4. Top evenly with the slivered almonds and mandarin oranges.

Tropical Island Salad

1 cup coconut milk

1 tablespoon agave nectar

1 tablespoon ground flaxseed

2 tablespoons chia seeds

2 cups unsweetened shredded coconut

1 cup chopped walnuts

4 cups pineapple chunks

1. In a blender, combine the coconut milk, agave, ground flaxseed, and chia seeds. Blend until thoroughly combined and thick. Pour mixture into a large mixing bowl.

2. Add the shredded coconut and walnuts to the coconut milk mixture and toss to combine.

3. Add the pineapple chunks to the mixture, toss to combine, and plate equal amounts into two bowls.

Tomato, Mozzarella, and Spinach Salad

2 cups washed baby spinach leaves

1 cup chopped tomatoes

½ cup chopped fresh buffalo mozzarella

2 tablespoons extra-virgin olive oil

2 teaspoons dried basil

1. Set out two salad bowls and split the spinach evenly between the two.

2. Top each salad with half of the tomatoes and half of the mozzarella.

3. Drizzle the olive oil over the top of both salads and sprinkle with the dried basil.

Tex-Mex Salad

▶ SERVES 2

1 tablespoon extra-virgin olive oil
1 cup canned, rinsed, and drained black
　beans
1 cup corn kernels
1 cup chopped tomatoes
1 teaspoon cayenne pepper
1 teaspoon ground cumin
2 cups chopped romaine lettuce

1. In a large mixing bowl, combine the olive oil, black beans, corn, tomatoes, cayenne, and cumin and toss to coat.
2. Add the chopped romaine lettuce and toss to thoroughly combine.
3. Divide the salad evenly between two salad bowls and serve.

ANY SALAD CAN BE A MEAL

If you start getting really creative with your salads, you can start converting your favorite dishes into healthier versions. Take any cuisine—Asian, Italian, Mediterranean, Southern, or Mexican—and you can twist any favorite recipe into a salad recipe. Start with a bed of lettuce and then load on the ingredients. Whether the spices are what make the cuisine unique or the protein sources that make it great, throw them in a salad.

Roasted Fennel, Tomato, and Chickpea Toss

▶ SERVES 2

2 large fennel bulbs, cut into ¼" chunks
2 pints cherry tomatoes
2 tablespoons extra-virgin olive oil
1 teaspoon all-natural sea salt
1 teaspoon freshly ground black pepper
2 cups cooked chickpeas

1. Preheat oven or broiler to broil at 400°F. Line a baking sheet with tin foil, spread the fennel chunks and tomatoes in an even layer on pan, drizzle with olive oil, sprinkle with salt and pepper, and broil 15–20 minutes, turning as needed to prevent burning.

2. Once the tomatoes are popped and fennel is soft, remove the fennel and tomatoes from heat. Pour the tomatoes, fennel, and oil into a mixing bowl.

3. Add the chickpeas to the mixing bowl, toss to combine thoroughly, and plate equal amounts onto two serving dishes.

Tangy Three-Bean Salad

▶ SERVES 4

2 tablespoons olive oil
2 tablespoons red wine vinegar
2 tablespoons Italian seasoning
1 teaspoon all-natural sea salt
½ teaspoon freshly ground black pepper
1 cup quartered artichoke hearts
½ medium red bell pepper, seeded and chopped
1 cup drained and rinsed canned garbanzo beans
1 cup drained and rinsed canned red kidney beans
1 cup drained and rinsed canned pinto beans
2 cups endive leaves

1. In a large mixing bowl, combine the olive oil, vinegar, Italian seasoning, salt, and pepper and whisk to combine well.
2. Add artichoke hearts, bell pepper, and beans to mixture. Toss to coat, cover, and refrigerate minimum of 4–6 hours but as long as overnight.
3. Toss endive leaves gently with bean mixture and place equal amounts of salad on four serving dishes or salad bowls.

Spicy Southwestern Two-Bean Salad

▶ SERVES 6–8

1 (15-ounce) can black beans, drained and rinsed

1 (15-ounce) can kidney beans, drained and rinsed

1 medium red or yellow bell pepper, seeded and chopped

1 large tomato, diced

⅔ cup corn (fresh, canned, or frozen)

⅓ cup olive oil

¼ cup lime juice

½ teaspoon chili powder

½ teaspoon garlic powder

¼ teaspoon cayenne pepper

½ teaspoon salt

¼ cup chopped fresh cilantro

1 avocado, pitted, flesh removed, and diced

MAKE IT A PASTA SALAD

Guess what? This recipe can also double as another kind of salad. Just omit the avocado and add some cooked pasta and extra dressing to turn it into a high-protein Tex-Mex pasta salad! Have this salad for lunch or a light dinner, and take the rest for leftovers the next day.

1. In a large bowl, combine the black beans, kidney beans, bell pepper, tomato, and corn.

2. In a separate small bowl, whisk together the olive oil, lime juice, chili powder, garlic powder, cayenne, and salt.

3. Pour over bean mixture; toss to coat. Stir in fresh cilantro.

4. Chill at least 1 hour before serving to allow flavors to mingle.

5. Add avocado and gently toss again just before serving.

Bean and Couscous Salad

▶ SERVES 2

2 cups prepared couscous
1 cup white beans, soaked and drained
¼ cup chopped scallions
¼ cup sweet peas
2 tablespoons balsamic vinegar
1 tablespoon extra-virgin olive oil

1. In a large mixing bowl, combine the couscous, beans, scallions, and peas and blend thoroughly.
2. Add the balsamic and olive oil over the mix and toss to coat, combining well.
3. Serve hot or cold.

WHAT'S YOUR SALAD?

There's absolutely no reason why a salad has to be lettuce, tomato, and cucumber. When you start getting creative and figuring out exactly what it is you love about salads, you'll start craving them like any other favorite food. Maybe salty ingredients like olives, artichokes, and roasted red peppers call your name, or the sweet and crunchy combination of dried fruit and nuts does the trick. Whatever the case may be, you can figure out a great salad that does your body good and does your taste buds great!

Lemon-Scented Rice with Fruit Salsa Salad

▶ SERVES 2

2 cups cooked wild rice
1 tablespoon freshly grated lemon zest
¼ cup lemon juice (about 1 lemon), divided
¼ cup champagne vinegar
1 tablespoon organic maple syrup
2 cups fruit salsa

LEMONS' LIMONIN

Widely known for their high content of vitamin C, lemons contain an astounding phytochemical called limonin. Acting as a powerful anti-inflammatory and cancer-fighting property, limonin is a strong crusader in the fight for better health by protecting the cells in all of the body's systems rather than just one system or organ.

1. In a large mixing bowl, combine the cooked wild rice, lemon zest, and half of the lemon juice (about ⅛ cup). Allow flavors to marry about 15 minutes.

2. In a small mixing bowl, whisk together the remaining ⅛ cup lemon juice, champagne vinegar, and maple syrup until thoroughly combined.

3. Add the fruit salsa to the wild rice; toss to combine. Pour the lemon juice, vinegar, and maple syrup mixture over the fruit and rice and toss to coat.

4. Serve immediately.

Sesame and Soy Cole Slaw Salad

1 head napa cabbage, shredded

1 carrot, grated

2 green onions, chopped

1 medium red bell pepper, seeded and
sliced thin

2 tablespoons olive oil

2 tablespoons apple cider vinegar

2 teaspoons soy sauce

½ teaspoon sesame oil

2 tablespoons maple syrup

2 tablespoons sesame seeds (optional)

EAT YOUR CABBAGE

While cabbage may not be your favorite vegetable, it's a good one to work into your diet here and there. Because it's mild in flavor, it serves as a great base for soups, salads, and other dishes. It's also an excellent source of vitamin C.

1. Toss together the cabbage, carrot, green onions, and bell pepper in a large bowl.

2. In a separate small bowl, whisk together the olive oil, vinegar, soy sauce, sesame oil, and maple syrup until well combined.

3. Drizzle dressing over cabbage mixture, add sesame seeds, and toss well to combine.

Tempeh "Chicken" Salad

▶ SERVES 3 OR 4

1 package tempeh, diced small

3 tablespoons vegan mayonnaise

2 teaspoons lemon juice

½ teaspoon garlic powder

1 teaspoon Dijon mustard

2 tablespoons sweet pickle relish

½ cup green peas

2 stalks celery, diced small

1 tablespoon chopped fresh dill
(optional)

TRY CURRIED "CHICKEN" TEMPEH

For curried chicken tempeh salad, omit the dill and add half a teaspoon curry powder and a dash cayenne and black pepper. If you don't feel up to dicing and simmering tempeh, try combining the dressing with store-bought mock chicken, or even veggie turkey or deli slices.

1. Cover tempeh with water in a small saucepan and simmer 10 minutes until tempeh is soft. Drain and allow to cool completely.

2. In a medium bowl, whisk together mayonnaise, lemon juice, garlic powder, mustard, and relish.

3. Add tempeh, peas, celery, and dill to mayonnaise mixture and gently toss to combine.

4. Chill at least 1 hour before serving to allow flavors to combine.

SOUPS AND STEWS

Mushroom Vegetable Stock

▶ MAKES ABOUT 6 CUPS

1 ounce dried mushrooms, such as porcini or Chinese black mushrooms
1 tablespoon olive oil
1 medium onion, peeled and sliced
1 medium carrot, peeled and sliced
2 stalks celery, roughly chopped
1 package (8–10 ounces) white mushrooms, washed and roughly chopped
3 cloves garlic, peeled and sliced
4 cups cold water
Small bunch of parsley stems
10 black peppercorns
8 sprigs fresh thyme
1 bay leaf
2 teaspoons salt

In a large bowl, soak the mushrooms in 4 cups water 1 hour. Heat the oil in a large stockpot; add onion, carrot, and celery. Cook over medium heat until onions begin to brown, about 15 minutes. Add the soaked mushrooms, their soaking liquid, the fresh white mushrooms, garlic, water, parsley stems, peppercorns, thyme, bay leaf, and salt. Bring to a boil, then lower heat. Simmer 45 minutes; strain. Keeps refrigerated for 1 week. Freezes well.

Vegetable Stock

▶ MAKES ABOUT 4 CUPS

1 medium onion, peeled and sliced
1 medium leek, white part only, cleaned thoroughly and sliced
1 medium carrot, peeled and sliced
2 stalks celery, roughly chopped
1 medium turnip, peeled and sliced
5 cloves garlic, peeled and sliced
6 cups cold water
Small bunch of parsley stems
10 black peppercorns
8 sprigs fresh thyme
1 bay leaf

Combine all ingredients in a large stockpot. Simmer 1 hour; strain. Season with salt and pepper if desired; cool. Keeps refrigerated for 1 week. Freezes well.

Ten-Minute Cheater's Chili

▶ SERVES 4 OR 5

1 (12-ounce) jar salsa
1 (14-ounce) can diced tomatoes
2 (14-ounce) cans kidney beans or black beans, rinsed and drained
1½ cups frozen veggies
4 veggie burgers, crumbled (optional)
2 tablespoons chili powder
1 teaspoon ground cumin
½ cup water

In a large pot, combine all ingredients. Simmer 10 minutes, stirring frequently.

THE MANY LIVES OF VEGGIE BURGERS

Don't believe the hype: veggie burgers don't have to always sit on buns! They're also great when crumbled up in soups and stews, like this one, or when used as an ingredient in omelets and lots of other recipes. Don't be afraid to get creative!

Veggie Crumble Chili

▶ SERVES 6

1 tablespoon vegetable oil

1 cup diced yellow onions

1 cup bell diced peppers

½ cup diced celery

1 tablespoon roasted garlic

3 (8-ounce) packets Boca Veggie Ground Crumbles

1 (1.25-ounce) packet chili seasoning mix

4 cups canned chili beans, undrained

1 (10-ounce) can milder diced tomatoes and green chilies, undrained

1 cup tomato sauce

½ teaspoon all-purpose seasoning

1. Spray a large saucepan with nonstick cooking spray. Add oil, onion, pepper, celery, and garlic. Cook on medium-high heat 6–8 minutes or until veggies have browned, stirring often.

2. Reduce heat to medium and add Boca Veggie Ground Crumbles to saucepan. Cook an additional 5–7 minutes.

3. Add remaining ingredients to saucepan and bring to a boil, stirring often. Simmer an additional 10–12 minutes or until thoroughly cooked.

Vegan Chili

SERVES 8

¼ cup olive oil

2 cups chopped onions

1 cup chopped carrots

2 cups chopped assorted bell peppers

2 teaspoons salt

1 tablespoon chopped garlic

2 small jalapeño peppers, seeded and chopped

1 tablespoon ground ancho chili pepper or ½ teaspoon crushed red pepper

1 chipotle in adobo, chopped

1 tablespoon toasted cumin seeds, ground, or 4 teaspoons ground cumin toasted briefly in a dry pan

1 (28-ounce) can plum tomatoes, roughly chopped, juice included

1 (16-ounce) can red kidney beans, rinsed and drained

1 (16-ounce) can cannellini beans, rinsed and drained

1 (16-ounce) can black beans, rinsed and drained

1 cup tomato juice

Finely chopped red onions for garnish

Chopped fresh cilantro for garnish

1. Heat the oil in a heavy-bottomed Dutch oven or soup pot. Add the onions, carrots, bell peppers, and salt; cook 15 minutes over medium heat until the onions are soft. Add the garlic, jalapeños, ancho, chipotle, and cumin; cook 5 minutes more.

2. Stir in tomatoes, beans, and tomato juice. Simmer about 45 minutes. Serve garnished with red onions and cilantro.

Golden West Chili

▶ SERVES 6

3 tablespoons vegetable oil

1 large onion, peeled and diced

12 ounces ground soy "meat" crumbles

1 tablespoon chili powder or more to taste

1 (15-ounce) can golden hominy

1 (15.5-ounce) can canary beans, drained and rinsed

1 (15.5-ounce) can pigeon peas, drained and rinsed

1 cup green salsa

1 cup Mexican beer or more as needed

Salt and freshly ground black pepper to taste

3 tomatillos, chopped

Grated Cheddar cheese

Chopped fresh cilantro

Diced avocados

Toasted pumpkin seeds

WHAT IS HOMINY?

If you are not from the South nor have ever eaten that Mexican classic posole, you may not be familiar with the white corn kernel known as hominy. Made from dried corn kernels that have been treated chemically, hominy has a pleasant texture and mild taste. In the Southwest and in Mexico, larger-kernel hominy is available and is known as posole. The smaller hominy is sold canned in most supermarkets; look for the larger variety at a Latino market.

1. Heat the oil in a large saucepan over medium heat and sauté the onion until partially golden, about 5 minutes. Add the soy "meat" crumbles and continue cooking 3–4 more minutes. Stir in the chili powder. Add the hominy, beans, pigeon peas, salsa, and beer and stir well.

2. Reduce the heat to medium-low and continue cooking and stirring about 8 minutes more. Season with salt and pepper. Serve in individual bowls; top with tomatillos, cheese, cilantro, avocado, and pumpkin seeds.

Five-Pepper Chili

> SERVES 8

1 medium onion, peeled and diced
1 small jalapeño, seeded and minced
1 small habanero pepper, seeded and minced
1 medium red bell pepper, seeded and diced
1 medium poblano pepper, seeded and diced
2 cloves garlic, peeled and minced
2 (15-ounce) cans crushed tomatoes
2 cups diced fresh tomatoes
2 tablespoons chili powder
1 tablespoon ground cumin
$\frac{1}{2}$ tablespoon cayenne pepper
$\frac{1}{8}$ cup vegan Worcestershire sauce
2 (15-ounce) cans pinto beans
1 teaspoon salt
$\frac{1}{4}$ teaspoon black pepper

In a 4-quart slow cooker, add all ingredients. Cover and cook on low heat 5 hours.

Jamaican Red Bean Stew

▶ SERVES 4

2 tablespoons olive oil
½ medium onion, peeled and diced
2 garlic cloves, minced
1 (15-ounce) can diced tomatoes
3 cups diced sweet potatoes
2 (15-ounce) cans red kidney beans, rinsed and drained
1 cup coconut milk
3 cups vegetable broth
2 teaspoons jerk seasoning
2 teaspoons curry powder
Salt and freshly ground black pepper to taste

1. In a small sauté pan over medium heat, add the olive oil, then sauté the onion and garlic about 3 minutes.

2. In a 4-quart slow cooker, add all ingredients. Cover and cook on low heat 6 hours.

Mediterranean Stew

▶ SERVES 4

3 tablespoons olive oil

3 cloves garlic, peeled, crushed, and minced

1 (15.5-ounce) can chickpeas, drained and rinsed

1 (19-ounce) can cannellini beans, drained and rinsed

2 cups roasted tomatoes

1½ cups quartered artichoke hearts

1 cup vegetable broth

4 tablespoons grated Parmesan cheese

1 teaspoon crushed red pepper or to taste

1 teaspoon dried oregano

Salt and freshly ground black pepper to taste

Chopped sun-dried tomatoes

Chopped fresh Italian parsley

Garlic-seasoned croutons

Crumbled feta cheese

Fresh oregano leaves

1. Heat the olive oil in a large saucepan over medium heat and sauté the garlic 2–3 minutes or until golden.

2. Reduce the heat to medium-low. Stir in the chickpeas, cannellini beans, roasted tomatoes, artichoke hearts, broth, Parmesan cheese, crushed red pepper, oregano, salt, and black pepper. Cook and stir about 10 minutes.

3. Serve in individual bowls; garnish with sun-dried tomatoes, parsley, croutons, feta, and oregano.

Cream of Asparagus Soup

▶ SERVES 6

2 tablespoons olive oil

1 medium onion, peeled and chopped

4 cloves garlic, peeled and finely chopped

1 pound fresh asparagus, roughly chopped

1 teaspoon salt

3 cups Vegetable Stock (see recipe in this chapter) or water

1 (10-ounce) package frozen green peas

2 cups cream or half-and-half

¼ teaspoon freshly ground black pepper or to taste

1 teaspoon dried basil

WITH ASPARAGUS, THIN AIN'T ALWAYS IN

Fat-n-sweet or thin and delicate, asparagus is one of the most sensuously delicious foods known to man. Contrary to popular belief, thick, voluptuous asparagus are not always woody and tough. In fact, they can have much more natural juiciness, sweetness, and silky texture than the pencil-thin variety. Check the cut bottoms of asparagus for freshness, making sure they're plump, moist, and recently cut. Wrinkled asparagus of any girth are no good.

1. In a large heavy-bottomed pot over medium heat, heat olive oil 1 minute. Add onion, garlic, asparagus, and salt; cook 15 minutes until onions are translucent but not browned. Add the stock. Simmer 20 minutes until asparagus is very tender. Remove from heat; stir in frozen peas.

2. Purée in a blender or food processor until smooth; transfer back to pot and heat just to a simmer. Add cream; season with salt, black pepper, and basil. May be served hot or cold.

Cream of Broccoli Soup

▶ SERVES 4

3 cups unsweetened almond milk
2 teaspoons all-natural sea salt
2 teaspoons garlic powder
1 teaspoon freshly ground black pepper
2 pounds broccoli florets
1 cup plain low-fat Greek-style yogurt or soy yogurt

1. In a large pot over medium heat, bring the almond milk, salt, garlic powder, pepper, and broccoli to a boil. Reduce heat to low and simmer 10–12 minutes.

2. Remove from heat and chill 5 minutes. Using an immersion blender, emulsify the broccoli mixture until no bits remain.

3. Add yogurt ¼ cup at a time and continue blending with the immersion blender until well blended. Serve hot or cold.

Cashew Cream of Asparagus Soup

▶ SERVES 4

1 onion, peeled and chopped

4 cloves garlic, peeled and minced

2 tablespoons olive oil

2 pounds asparagus, trimmed and chopped

4 cups vegetable broth

¾ cup raw cashews

¾ cup water

¼ teaspoon ground sage

½ teaspoon salt

¼ teaspoon freshly ground black pepper

2 teaspoons lemon juice

2 tablespoons nutritional yeast (optional)

VARIETIES OF VEGGIE BROTHS

A basic vegetable broth is made by simmering vegetables, potatoes, and a bay leaf or two in water at least 30 minutes. While you may be familiar with the canned and boxed stocks available at the grocery store, vegan chefs have a few other tricks up their sleeves to impart extra flavor to recipes calling for vegetable broth. Check your natural grocer for specialty flavored bouillon cubes such as vegetarian "chicken" or "beef" flavor, or shop the bulk bins for powdered vegetable broth mix.

1. In a large soup or stockpot, sauté onion and garlic in olive oil over medium heat 2–3 minutes until onion is soft. Reduce heat and carefully add asparagus and vegetable broth.

2. Bring to a simmer, cover, and cook 20 minutes. Cool slightly, then purée in a blender, working in batches as needed until almost smooth. Return to pot over low heat.

3. In a blender or food processor, purée cashews and water until smooth and add to soup. Add sage, salt, and pepper and heat a few more minutes, stirring to combine.

4. Stir in lemon juice and nutritional yeast just before serving and adjust seasonings to taste.

Cream of Carrot Soup with Coconut

▶ SERVES 6

3 medium carrots, peeled and chopped

1 medium sweet potato, peeled and chopped

1 medium yellow onion, peeled and chopped

3½ cups vegetable broth

3 cloves garlic, peeled and minced

2 teaspoons minced fresh ginger

1 (14-ounce) can coconut milk

1 teaspoon salt

¼ teaspoon ground cinnamon (optional)

> **EAT CARROTS FOR YOUR EYES**
>
> In addition to being crunchy and tasty, carrots are also really good for you. They're rich in dietary fiber, antioxidants, and minerals, as well as vitamin A, which helps maintain your vision. An urban legend says that eating large amounts of carrots will allow you to see in the dark! While this isn't exactly true, it is a good indicator that you should work more carrots into your diet.

1. In a large soup or stockpot, bring the carrots, sweet potato, and onion to a simmer in the vegetable broth. Add garlic and ginger, cover, and heat 20–25 minutes until carrots and potatoes are soft.

2. Allow to cool slightly, then transfer to a blender and purée until smooth.

3. Return soup to pot. Over very low heat, stir in the coconut milk and salt, stirring well to combine. Heat just until heated through, another 3–4 minutes.

4. Garnish with cinnamon just before serving.

Clean Creamy Zucchini Soup

▶ SERVES 6

1 tablespoon extra-virgin olive oil

1 large Vidalia onion, peeled and sliced

2 cups Vegetable Stock (see recipe in this chapter), divided

2 pounds zucchini, rinsed and sliced

2 cloves garlic, peeled and minced

1 teaspoon all-natural sea salt

1 teaspoon freshly ground black pepper

1 teaspoon Italian seasoning

2 cups nonfat Greek-style yogurt or soy yogurt

ZUCCHINI: A BLANK CANVAS

Aside from all of the valuable nutrients like vitamins B6 and C, minerals like magnesium and folate, and amazing antioxidants that all combine to protect and improve your health, zucchini has the added benefit of being able to absorb the flavors of any dish. Much like a blank canvas, zucchini can be painted with flavors from foods or spices to provide a unique crunch or softness to any dish but with the flavors of other powerful ingredients.

1. In a large pot over medium heat, warm the olive oil and add the sliced onions. Sauté 4–5 minutes or until onions are soft and translucent.

2. Add 3 tablespoons stock, the zucchini, garlic, salt, pepper, and Italian seasoning to the pot. Sauté 10–12 minutes or until zucchini is soft.

3. Add the remaining stock, bring to a boil, reduce heat to low, and simmer 25–30 minutes.

4. Remove the pot from heat and allow soup to cool 15–20 minutes. Using an immersion blender, emulsify the ingredients to desired chunkiness. Gradually stir in the yogurt ½ cup at a time until desired thickness and texture is achieved.

Barley Vegetable Soup

▶ SERVES 6

1 medium onion, peeled and chopped

2 medium carrots, peeled and sliced

2 ribs celery, chopped

2 tablespoons olive oil

8 cups vegetable broth

1 cup barley

1½ cups frozen mixed vegetables

1 (14-ounce) can crushed or diced tomatoes

½ teaspoon dried parsley

½ teaspoon dried thyme

2 bay leaves

Salt and freshly ground black pepper to taste

1. In a large soup or stockpot, sauté the onion, carrot, and celery in olive oil 3–5 minutes over medium heat just until onions are almost soft.

2. Reduce heat to medium-low and add remaining ingredients except salt and pepper.

3. Bring to a simmer, cover, and cook at least 45 minutes, stirring occasionally.

4. Remove cover and cook 10 more minutes.

5. Remove bay leaves; season with salt and pepper to taste.

Carrot Purée with Nutmeg

► SERVES 6

2 tablespoons oil

1 medium onion, peeled and chopped

4 cups carrots, peeled, halved lengthwise, and sliced thin

2 cups Vegetable Stock (see recipe in this chapter)

1 teaspoon salt

Ground white pepper to taste

Pinch of ground nutmeg

1¼ cups milk

2 teaspoons chopped fresh chives or parsley

1. Heat oil in large saucepan over medium-high heat. Add onion and sauté 5 minutes, then add carrots. Cook 1 minute.

2. Add stock, salt, pepper, and nutmeg. Bring to a boil, then reduce to simmer 20 minutes.

3. Ladle into a blender, add 1 cup milk, and blend until very smooth. Adjust consistency with more milk if necessary. Be careful when puréeing the hot liquid; start the blender on the slowest speed and/or do the job in two batches. Serve garnished with a sprinkling of chives or parsley.

Chilled Curry Potato-Fennel Soup

1 tablespoon olive oil

1 large Idaho russet potato, peeled and coarsely chopped

1 large Spanish onion, peeled and coarsely chopped

1 head sweet fennel, tassel-like fronds removed and set aside, bulb
coarsely chopped

1 medium red bell pepper, seeded and coarsely chopped

1 (1") piece fresh ginger, peeled and finely chopped

2 cloves garlic, peeled and finely chopped

2 teaspoons good-quality Madras curry powder

3 cups Vegetable Stock (see recipe in this chapter)

1 medium jalapeño pepper, seeded and finely chopped (optional)

1 quart buttermilk

1 cup half-and-half

Salt and white pepper to taste

1 tablespoon chopped fresh Italian parsley

1. In a large soup pot over medium-high heat, heat the oil 1 minute.
   Add the chopped vegetables, ginger, and garlic. Cook until onions are
   translucent, about 5 minutes; stir in curry powder and cook 5 minutes
   more. Add vegetable stock; raise heat to high and bring to a full boil.
   Reduce to a simmer; cook until potatoes are falling-apart tender, about
   15 minutes.

2. Chill and purée the soup in a blender or food processor. Add the
   chopped jalapeño, buttermilk, and half-and-half. Season to taste with
   salt and white pepper. Serve garnished with chopped parsley and/or
   sprigs from the reserved fennel fronds.

Clean French Onion Soup

▶ SERVES 4

¼ cup olive oil
4 large Vidalia onions, peeled and sliced
4 cloves garlic, peeled and minced
1 tablespoon dried thyme
½ cup Worcestershire sauce
4½ cups Vegetable Stock (see recipe in this chapter)
1 teaspoon all-natural sea salt
1 teaspoon freshly ground black pepper
4 slices 100% whole-wheat French bread
4 ounces buffalo mozzarella or vegan mozzarella

1. In a small sauté pan, heat the olive oil over medium-high heat and cook the onions until golden brown, about 3 minutes. Add the garlic and sauté 1 minute.

2. In a 4-quart slow cooker, pour the sautéed vegetables, thyme, Worcestershire, stock, salt, and pepper. Cover and cook on low heat 4 hours.

3. While the soup is cooking, preheat the oven to the broiler setting. Lightly toast the slices of French bread.

4. To serve, ladle the soup into four broiler-safe bowls, place a slice of the toasted French bread on top of each bowl, put a slice of the mozzarella cheese on top of the bread, and place the bowls under the broiler until the cheese has melted.

Gazpacho

8 medium tomatoes, seeded and roughly chopped
1 large cucumber, peeled and roughly chopped
2 medium green bell peppers, seeded and roughly chopped
1 slice bread, torn into postage-stamp-sized pieces
1 clove garlic, peeled and sliced
2 tablespoons extra-virgin olive oil
1½ teaspoons red wine vinegar
1 teaspoon salt
1–2 cups tomato juice
Hot pepper sauce (optional)

Combine the tomatoes, cucumber, peppers, bread, garlic, olive oil, vinegar, and salt in a food processor or blender. Purée at high speed until consistency is soupy but still slightly chunky. Stir in tomato juice to desired consistency and season with hot pepper sauce to taste.

Indian Curried Lentil Soup

▶ SERVES 4

1 medium onion, peeled and diced
1 medium carrot, peeled and sliced
3 whole cloves
2 tablespoons vegan margarine
1 teaspoon ground cumin
1 teaspoon ground turmeric
1 cup yellow or green lentils
2¾ cups vegetable broth
2 large tomatoes, chopped
1 teaspoon salt
¼ teaspoon freshly ground black pepper
1 teaspoon lemon juice

1. In a large soup or stockpot over medium heat, sauté the onion, carrot, and cloves in margarine until onions are just turning soft, about 3 minutes. Add cumin and turmeric and toast 1 minute, stirring constantly to avoid burning.

2. Reduce heat to medium-low and add lentils, vegetable broth, tomatoes, and salt. Bring to a simmer, cover, and cook 35–40 minutes or until lentils are done.

3. Season with black pepper and lemon juice just before serving.

Lentil-Vegetable Soup

▶ SERVES 8

1 tablespoon extra-virgin olive oil
½ cup chopped yellow onion
½ cup diced carrot
½ cup diced celery
2 cloves garlic, peeled and minced
2 teaspoons dried Italian seasoning
1 bay leaf
2 cups dry lentils
4 cups Vegetable Stock (see recipe in this chapter)
4 cups water
2 large tomatoes, peeled, cored, and chopped
½ cup baby spinach leaves, rinsed
1 teaspoon all-natural sea salt
½ teaspoon freshly ground black pepper

1. Pour olive oil into a large pot over medium heat. After oil runs thin, add the onion, carrots, and celery and sauté 5 minutes or until tender but not burned. Add the garlic, Italian seasoning, and bay leaf and sauté about 1 minute before adding the lentils, stock, water, and tomatoes.

2. Bring pot to a boil, reduce heat, and simmer soup uncovered about 1 hour.

3. Before removing from heat, add spinach, salt, and pepper and stir until spinach is wilted.

Lentil Soup with Cumin

▶ SERVES 8

1 tablespoon olive oil

1 large carrot peeled and cut into bite-sized pieces

1 stalk celery cut into bite-sized pieces

1 medium onion, peeled and chopped into bite-sized pieces

1 medium potato, peeled and chopped into bite-sized pieces

2 cloves garlic, peeled and thinly sliced

½ teaspoon whole cumin seeds, toasted in a dry pan 1 minute until
  fragrant

2 teaspoons salt plus more to taste

1 cup lentils

8 cups Vegetable Stock (see recipe in this chapter)

Freshly ground black pepper to taste

1. Heat the oil over medium heat in a pot large enough to hold
   everything and add the vegetables, garlic, cumin, and 2 teaspoons salt.
   Cook 5 minutes, then add the lentils and vegetable stock. Raise heat to
   bring to a boil, then reduce heat to medium-low.

2. Simmer 1 hour, season with salt and pepper, and serve warm.

Minestrone with Pesto

▶ SERVES 10–12

1 tablespoon olive oil

2 stalks celery, cut into ¼" dice

1 large carrot, peeled and cut into ¼" dice

1 medium potato, peeled and cut into ¼" dice

1 medium zucchini, cut into ¼" dice

1 medium yellow "summer" squash, cut into ¼" dice

1 large Spanish onion, peeled and cut into ¼" dice

2 leeks, washed and chopped

3 cloves garlic, peeled and finely chopped

1 teaspoon salt

3 teaspoons chopped fresh oregano or 1 teaspoon dried oregano leaves

3 teaspoons chopped fresh thyme or 1 teaspoon dried thyme leaves

1 bay leaf

2 quarts Vegetable Stock (see recipe in this chapter) or water

1 (30-ounce) can diced tomatoes

2 cups cooked pasta (any small shape, such as ditalini)

1 (14-ounce) can red kidney or white cannellini beans

Salt and white pepper to taste

4 tablespoons store-bought pesto

Grated Parmesan cheese (optional)

1. In a large soup pot or Dutch oven over medium-high heat, heat the olive oil 1 minute. Add all diced vegetables, leeks, garlic, salt, oregano, thyme, and bay leaf. Cook 10–15 minutes until onions turn translucent. Add stock and tomatoes. Bring to a full boil; reduce heat to a simmer and cook 45 minutes until potatoes are cooked through and tender.

2. Add cooked pasta and beans. Bring back to a boil 1 minute; season to taste with salt and white pepper. Serve in bowls topped with a teaspoon of pesto. Pass grated Parmesan cheese at the table if desired.

Pumpkin Soup with Caraway Seeds

▶ SERVES 4

2 tablespoons unsalted butter or olive oil
1 medium onion, peeled and chopped
1 large carrot, peeled and sliced thin
2 cups peeled, cubed pumpkin
¼ teaspoon whole caraway seeds
1½ cups Vegetable Stock (see recipe in this chapter)
3 cups cold milk
Salt and freshly ground black pepper to taste
½ teaspoon dried chipotle chili or smoked Spanish paprika

1. Melt the butter or heat the olive oil in a heavy-bottomed soup pot over medium heat. Add the onion, carrot, pumpkin, and caraway seeds and sauté stirring occasionally 8–10 minutes until pumpkin becomes tender and begins to brown (some may stick to pan).

2. Add stock (or broth) and simmer 20 minutes. Remove from heat and stir in 2 cups milk.

3. Purée in batches in a blender until smooth, adjusting consistency with remaining milk. Season with salt and pepper to taste. Sprinkle the chipotle chili or Spanish paprika on top.

Curried Pumpkin Bisque

▶ SERVES 4

4 cups pumpkin purée
2½ cups coconut milk
3 teaspoons curry powder
1 teaspoon all-natural sea salt
1 teaspoon freshly ground black pepper

1. In a large pot over medium heat, whisk together the pumpkin purée and coconut milk. Add curry and combine thoroughly.

2. Heat through 5–7 minutes and remove from heat.

3. Add sea salt and black pepper.

THE "GOOD-FOR-YOU" STARCH IN PUMPKIN

While early researchers who studied carbohydrates like breads, potatoes, and pastas warned consumers to beware of foods high in starch because of their effects on blood sugar and the waistline, recent research has shown that the source of starch is far more important than the starch itself. Pumpkin and other winter squash have actually been deemed as beneficial starches because they produce phytochemicals called pectins that contain a specific acid called homogalacturonan. This acid acts as a triple-threat to fending off disease by promoting health of cells as an antioxidant; preventing cell damage as an anti-inflammatory agent; and stabilizing blood sugar with its ability to regulate blood insulin.

Pumpkin-Ale Soup

▶ SERVES 6

2 (15-ounce) cans pumpkin purée
¼ cup diced onion
2 cloves garlic, peeled and minced
2 teaspoons salt
1 teaspoon freshly ground black pepper
¼ teaspoon dried thyme
5 cups vegetable broth
1 (12-ounce) bottle pale ale beer

1. In a 4-quart slow cooker, add the pumpkin purée, onion, garlic, salt, pepper, thyme, and vegetable broth. Stir well. Cover and cook over low heat 4 hours.

2. Allow the soup to cool slightly, then process in a blender or with an immersion blender until smooth.

3. Pour the soup back into the slow cooker, add the beer, and cook 1 hour over low heat.

Red Bean and Pasta Soup

▶ SERVES 8

1 medium onion, peeled and chopped

3 cloves garlic, peeled and sliced

3 tablespoons olive oil

1 teaspoon dried oregano

2 bay leaves

1 (8-ounce) can tomato sauce

2 teaspoons salt

1 tablespoon soy sauce

1 (16-ounce) package red beans, soaked overnight in 1 quart cold water
    and drained

10 sprigs Italian parsley, including stems

6 cups Vegetable Stock (see recipe in this chapter) or water

2 cups cooked pasta (any small shape, such as orzo or ditalini)

Sour cream (optional for garnish)

1. In a pot large enough to hold all ingredients, cook onions and garlic
   with olive oil over medium heat 5 minutes until onions are translucent.
   Add oregano, bay leaves, tomato sauce, salt, and soy sauce. Bring to a
   simmer and add beans, parsley, and stock (or water).

2. Bring to a boil, then reduce to a low simmer and cook 90 minutes
   until beans are tender enough to mash between two fingers. In a
   blender, purée ⅓ of the beans very well; add them back to the soup.
   Add cooked pasta and bring back to a boil 1 minute more before
   serving garnished with a dollop of sour cream if desired.

Smoky Black-Eyed Pea Soup with Sweet Potatoes and Mustard Greens

▶ SERVES 10–12

1 tablespoon olive oil

1 medium onion, peeled and chopped

2 ribs celery, chopped

1 medium carrot, peeled and chopped

2 teaspoons salt plus more to taste

1 teaspoon dried thyme

2 teaspoons dried oregano

1 teaspoon ground cumin

1 dried chipotle chili, halved

2 bay leaves

1 pound dried black-eyed peas or navy beans, washed and picked through for stones

2 quarts Vegetable Stock (see recipe in this chapter) or water

1 large sweet potato, peeled and diced into 1" cubes

1 (10-ounce) package frozen mustard greens, chopped

1 (22-ounce) can diced tomatoes

Freshly ground black pepper to taste

Croutons of corn bread or other bread for garnish

Chopped cilantro for garnish

USING SMOKED CHILIES OR SPICES TO ADD SMOKY FLAVOR

For a smoky flavor, nonvegetarian recipes often call for smoked pork bones or bacon. Vegetarians can achieve a similar result by adding smoked chilies such as chipotles (smoked jalapeños) to those dishes.

1. In a large heavy-bottomed Dutch oven over medium heat, heat the oil 1 minute. Add onion, celery, carrot, and salt; cook 5 minutes until onions are translucent. Add thyme, oregano, cumin, chipotle chili, and bay leaves; cook 2 minutes more. Add black-eyed peas and vegetable stock.

2. Bring to a boil, then simmer 2 hours until beans are very tender, adding water or stock if necessary.

3. Add the sweet potatoes and cook 20 minutes more. Stir in chopped mustard greens and diced tomatoes. Cook 10 minutes more until the potatoes and greens are tender. Adjust seasoning with salt and pepper, and consistency with additional vegetable stock or water. The soup should be brothy. Serve garnished with corn bread croutons and a sprinkling of chopped cilantro.

Smooth Cauliflower Soup with Coriander

SERVES 4–6

2 tablespoons unsalted butter or olive oil
1 medium onion, peeled and chopped
1 medium head (about 2 pounds) cauliflower, cut into bite-sized pieces
2 cups Vegetable Stock (see recipe in this chapter)
1 teaspoon salt
½ teaspoon ground white pepper
1 teaspoon ground coriander
¾ cup cold milk
Chopped fresh chives or parsley

1. In a large saucepan or soup pot over medium-high heat, melt butter or heat oil. Add onion; cook until it is translucent but not brown, about 5 minutes. Add cauliflower; cook 1 minute. Add the stock, salt, pepper, and coriander; bring up to a rolling boil.

2. Simmer until cauliflower is very tender, about 15 minutes. Transfer to a blender. Add half of the milk and purée until very smooth, scraping down the sides of the blender vase with a rubber spatula. Be very careful during this step, since hot liquids will splash out of blender if it is not started gradually (you may wish to purée in two batches, for safety). Transfer soup back to saucepan and thin with additional milk if necessary. Season; garnish with chopped herbs just before serving.

Saucy Southwestern Soup

▶ SERVES 6

1 medium yellow onion, peeled and chopped

1 cup chopped celery

1 teaspoon garlic powder

1 tablespoon minced fresh jalapeño (optional)

½ teaspoon cayenne pepper

1 teaspoon chopped fresh cilantro

6 cups Vegetable Stock (see recipe in this chapter), divided

2 cups refried beans

1 cup chopped tomatoes

1 cup fresh or frozen corn kernels

1 teaspoon all-natural sea salt

½ teaspoon freshly ground black pepper

1. In a large pot, combine the onion, celery, garlic powder, jalapeño, cayenne, cilantro, and ¼ cup stock. Sauté about 2 minutes or until vegetables are only slightly tender.

2. Add the remaining stock, refried beans, tomatoes, corn, salt, and pepper and bring to a boil. Reduce heat to low and allow soup to simmer 10–15 minutes or until corn is cooked through and flavors are married.

Spicy Sweet Potato Soup

▶ SERVES 4

3 cups water

2 medium sweet potatoes, peeled, rinsed, and cut into ¼" slices

½ teaspoon cayenne pepper, divided

½ teaspoon all-natural sea salt, divided

1. In a medium pot over medium-high heat, add water and sweet potatoes and bring to a boil.

2. Reduce heat to simmer and cook until sweet potatoes are fork-tender. Remove from heat and reserve water from pot in a separate measuring cup.

3. Sprinkle sweet potatoes with ¼ teaspoon cayenne and ¼ teaspoon salt and add ¼ cup of removed water back to pot.

4. Using an immersion blender, emulsify potatoes, adding removed water as needed until desired thickness is achieved.

5. While emulsifying, add remaining cayenne and salt.

BOIL OR BAKE SWEET POTATOES FOR BETTER NUTRITION

With a number of studies focusing on determining which foods provide the best nutritional values, more studies are focusing on the benefits of the manner in which those foods are prepared. By testing the nutrition content of foods in their natural state (raw), and then again after cooking them in a variety of methods, researchers have been able to identify which cooking methods maintain, promote, or deteriorate the nutrients of those foods. Sweet potatoes, for example, have been found to hold most of their nutritional value through the process of baking or boiling, while steaming has been determined to undermine the vitamin A levels.

Tomato Soup

▶ SERVES 6

2 tablespoons olive oil

1 medium onion, peeled and chopped

2 cloves garlic, peeled and finely
    chopped

4 pounds ripe tomatoes, peeled, seeded,
    and roughly chopped

1 teaspoon salt

Freshly ground black pepper to taste
    (about ¼ teaspoon)

**SMOOTH MOVES:
BLENDER VERSUS
FOOD PROCESSOR**

They seem interchangeable sometimes, but they're not. Blenders and food processors are different tools with different strengths. For ultrasmooth purées, a blender is the first choice. For rougher purées, or chopping jobs with drier ingredients, use a processor.

1. In a large soup pot over medium heat, heat olive oil 1 minute. Add onion and garlic; cook 5–10 minutes until onions are translucent but not browned. Stir in tomatoes; simmer 25–30 minutes until tomatoes are submerged in their own juices.

2. Purée in a blender or food processor until smooth. Season with salt and black pepper. May be served hot or cold. Add cream if desired for cream of tomato soup.

Creamy Tomato-Basil Soup

▷ SERVES 4

1 cup water
10 medium tomatoes
1 cup chopped fresh basil
1 tablespoon minced garlic
2 teaspoons all-natural sea salt
2 cups tomato sauce
1 cup plain Greek-style low-fat yogurt or soy yogurt

1. In a large pot, bring the water, tomatoes, basil, and garlic to a boil. Reduce heat to low and simmer 15–20 minutes. Allow to cool.

2. With an immersion blender, emulsify the tomatoes and spices completely until no bits remain.

3. Add the sea salt, tomato sauce, and the yogurt ¼ cup at a time and use the immersion blender to fully combine. Serve hot or cold.

Wild Mushroom Soup with Thyme

▶ SERVES 8

1 pound white mushrooms

½ pound shiitake mushrooms, stems removed

1 teaspoon olive oil

4 sprigs fresh thyme or ½ teaspoon dried

4 or 5 shallots, peeled and chopped very fine

Pinch of salt plus more to taste

¼ cup dry white wine

2 cups Vegetable Stock (see recipe in this chapter) or water

½ pound assorted wild mushrooms (chanterelle, shiitake, oyster, cremini, black trumpet, etc.), sliced into bite-sized pieces, or an equal amount of sliced white mushrooms

2 teaspoons butter

Freshly ground black pepper to taste

3 cups cold milk

1 tablespoon finely chopped fresh chives

1. Pulse the white mushrooms in about four small batches in a food processor to finely chop them, stopping before they clump. Roughly hand-chop the shiitakes, then pulse them the same way.

2. Heat the oil in a 2½-cup saucepan over medium-high heat; toss in the thyme and allow to sizzle for a moment, then add the shallots and sauté 3 minutes until translucent. Add the chopped mushrooms. Sprinkle in a pinch of salt and cook 5–7 minutes until mushrooms are soft.

3. Add white wine and cook 2 minutes, then add the stock. Simmer 10 minutes.

4. Meanwhile, in a medium sauté pan over high heat, sauté the sliced mushrooms in the butter in small batches, seasoning them with salt and pepper as they cook. Set aside.

5. Put ⅓ of soup in blender with 1 cup cold milk and purée until very smooth. Repeat with remaining soup and milk, then season to taste. Be careful to vent the blender to avoid dangerous splashing. Serve with a spoonful of sautéed mushrooms in each bowl and a sprinkling of chives.

Mushroom, Barley, and Collard Greens Soup

▶ SERVES 12

2 tablespoons olive oil

2 pounds mushrooms (any variety)

1 large onion, peeled and chopped

1 medium carrot, peeled and chopped

2 stalks celery, chopped

4 cloves garlic, peeled and roughly chopped

2 bay leaves

2 tablespoons fresh or 2 teaspoons dried marjoram or oregano

1½ teaspoons fresh or ½ teaspoon dried rosemary

2 teaspoons salt

½ teaspoon freshly ground black pepper

2 cups pearl barley, rinsed

3 quarts Vegetable Stock (see recipe in this chapter) or water

2 (10-ounce) packages frozen chopped collard greens

1. Heat the oil in a large soup pot over medium-high heat 1 minute. Add mushrooms, onions, carrot, celery, garlic, bay leaves, marjoram, rosemary, salt, and pepper. Cook until vegetables have softened significantly and are stewing in their natural broth, about 15 minutes.

2. Stir in barley and stock. Bring the soup up to a full boil, then reduce to a medium simmer and cook until barley is tender, about 40 minutes.

3. Add the collards; cook about 10 minutes more. Season to taste.

Vichyssoise (Potato and Leek Soup)

▶ SERVES 12

1 tablespoon olive oil

1 medium onion, peeled and chopped

1 pound (3 or 4) potatoes, any variety, peeled and cut into 1" chunks

2 bunches leeks, thoroughly washed and chopped; set aside 1 cup of the best parts for garnish

1 teaspoon dried sage

1 bay leaf

¼ cup white wine

2 quarts Vegetable Stock (see recipe in this chapter) or water

Salt and white pepper to taste

1. In a large soup pot over medium heat, heat olive oil 1 minute. Add onion, potatoes, and all but 1 cup of the chopped leeks; cook 10 minutes until onions turn translucent. Add sage, bay leaf, and wine. Cook 1 minute more. Add stock. Bring to a full boil; reduce heat to a simmer and cook 45 minutes until potatoes are very tender and starting to fall apart.

2. Carefully purée the soup in a blender in small batches. Season to taste with salt and white pepper. Steam, boil, or sauté the remaining 1 cup leeks, and serve the soup garnished with a spoonful of leeks in the center.

Yellow Split Pea Soup with Cactus and Hominy

▶ SERVES 12

1 tablespoon olive oil

1 medium onion, peeled and chopped

2 ribs celery, chopped

1 medium carrot, peeled and chopped

1 tablespoon dried marjoram or oregano

1 teaspoon ground cumin, toasted in a dry pan until fragrant

½ teaspoon ground coriander

1 bay leaf

1 pound dried yellow split peas

2 quarts Vegetable Stock (see recipe in this chapter) or water

2 ancho or guajillo chili pods, oven-toasted for 2 minutes at 350°F, seeded, boiled for 5 minutes in a cup of water, and puréed in a blender

1 tablespoon vegetable oil

1 (30-ounce) can hominy corn kernels, drained and rinsed

1 (15-ounce) can cactus (nopalitos), drained and rinsed

Salt and freshly ground black pepper to taste

Chopped cilantro for garnish

Croutons (optional)

1. In a large soup pot over medium heat, heat olive oil 1 minute. Add onion, celery, and carrot; cook 5 minutes until onions turn translucent. Add marjoram, cumin, coriander, and bay leaf. Cook 1 minute more. Add split peas and stock. Raise heat to high and bring to a full boil; reduce heat to a simmer. Add puréed chili and cook 45 minutes until peas are very tender and starting to fall apart.

2. Add hominy and cactus; bring back to a boil. Cook 1 minute more; season to taste with salt and pepper and remove from heat. Serve garnished with chopped cilantro and croutons.

Miso Soup

5 cups vegetable or mushroom stock

1 (5" square) piece kombu (kelp, a dried seaweed)

1 teaspoon soy sauce

3 tablespoons light miso, such as shinshu (yellow), shiro (white), or mugi (barley) miso

2 scallions, chopped

2 ounces firm tofu, diced into small cubes

4 teaspoons wakame seaweed (instant)

1. Bring stock and kombu to a boil in a soup pot. Cover; remove from heat and let stand 5 minutes. Strain; stir in soy sauce.

2. In a mixing bowl, mix about ¼ cup of the warm stock into the miso paste with a wire whisk until the miso is dissolved. Pour this mixture back into the remaining stock. Place scallions, diced tofu, and wakame into four bowls. Gently ladle soup into the bowls.

English Garden Pea Soup

▶ SERVES 2

1 tablespoon olive oil

2 cloves garlic, peeled and thinly sliced

1 medium leek, washed and thinly sliced

2 cups garden peas

1 cup white wine

3 tablespoons plain yogurt

3 tablespoons heavy cream (optional)

Salt and freshly ground black pepper to taste

Snipped chives

Garlic croutons

Soy bacon

Tarragon leaves

RINSING LEEKS

Because leeks are raised in mounds of sand, the grains of which seem to trickle freely between its tightly furled leaves in the stalk, leeks are notoriously gritty and require a thorough rinsing in cold water. One way to get rid of the sand is to slice from just above the root end (leave the root intact for this) and, using a very sharp knife, slit the leek in half lengthwise. Then swish the leek and its separated leaves through a sink of water. When the sand is gone, slice off the root and use.

1. Heat the olive oil in a medium saucepan over medium heat and sauté the garlic and leek 3–4 minutes.

2. Spoon this mixture into a blender or food processor. Add the peas, white wine, yogurt, and heavy cream if using. Purée until smooth. Season with salt and pepper.

3. Pour into soup bowls and garnish with chives, croutons, bacon, and tarragon leaves.

Corn and Potato Chowder

▶ SERVES 12

8 ears shucked sweet corn

1 tablespoon olive oil

2 large onions, peeled and chopped

2 stalks celery, chopped

1 pound red potatoes, cut into 1" chunks

3 sprigs fresh thyme or 1 teaspoon dried thyme

1 bay leaf

3 teaspoons salt

1 smoked chili (optional)

4 ounces (1 stick) unsalted butter

3 quarts Vegetable Stock (see recipe in this chapter) or water

4 teaspoons cornstarch dissolved in ¼ cup water

1 quart cream or milk

Ground white pepper and additional salt to taste

2 tablespoons chopped fresh parsley

BROTHY VERSUS THICK CHOWDERS

While generations of canned soups have conditioned us to believe that chowder is, by definition, a thick, pasty soup, some of the most delicious handmade versions of these chunky soups feature a thin, though rich, broth.

1. Cut corn kernels from the cob using a slicing motion with a kitchen knife. Reserve the cobs and set kernels aside.

2. In a large soup pot over medium-high heat, heat olive oil 1 minute. Add the corn cobs, onions, celery, potatoes, thyme, bay leaf, salt, and chili if using. Cook until onions are translucent, about 5 minutes. Add the butter and cook gently, allowing the vegetables to stew in the butter about 5 more minutes.

3. Add the vegetable stock. Raise heat to high and bring to a full boil. Lower to a simmer and cook 10 minutes more. Remove the corn cobs; add cornstarch mixture and corn kernels and simmer 5 minutes more. Stir in the cream and adjust seasoning with salt and white pepper. Serve sprinkled with parsley.

Acorn Squash Soup with Anise and Carrots

▶ SERVES 6

1 tablespoon olive oil

2 medium onions, peeled and chopped

1 teaspoon salt

1 medium acorn squash (about 2 pounds), peeled and cut into 1" chunks

2 large carrots, peeled and cut into 1" chunks

1 teaspoon anise seeds, toasted in a dry pan for 2 minutes until fragrant

¼ cup cognac or brandy

1 pint Vegetable Stock (see recipe in this chapter)

1–2 cups skim milk

Chopped fresh parsley

1. Heat the olive oil in a heavy medium saucepot over medium heat. Add the onions and salt; cook until translucent and slightly browned, about 10 minutes.

2. Lower heat to medium-low. Add the squash, carrots, and anise seeds; cook slowly, stirring the browned bits from the bottom of the pan frequently with a wooden spoon. These browned natural sugars will give the soup its caramelized complexity.

3. When the squash is soft and browned, add the cognac; cook 2 minutes to steam off the alcohol. Add the stock; simmer 15 minutes.

4. In a blender, purée the soup with as much skim milk as necessary for a thick but soupy consistency. Season to taste. Serve garnished with a sprinkling of chopped parsley.

White Bean Soup with Chipotle Croutons

▷ SERVES 4

2 (15.5-ounce) cans navy or other white beans, drained and rinsed

1½ cups fresh or canned tomatoes

1 teaspoon dried oregano

1 teaspoon chipotle sauce (adobo)

Salt and freshly ground black pepper to taste

2 tablespoons olive oil (4 tablespoons if using soy chorizo)

1 (12-ounce) package soy chorizo "sausage" (optional)

1 cup garlic croutons sprinkled with ground chipotle chilies

2 tablespoons diced red onion

Chopped fresh cilantro

1. Put 1 can beans into the blender or food processor. Add the tomatoes, oregano, chipotle sauce, salt and pepper, and 2 tablespoons olive oil and process until fairly smooth. Pour into a large saucepan.

2. If using the chorizo, heat 2 more tablespoons olive oil in a small skillet over medium-low heat and crumble and sauté the sausage.

3. Heat the soup in a saucepan over medium heat; stir in the remaining beans and the chorizo "sausage" if using. To serve, ladle soup into individual bowls and garnish with the croutons, red onions, and cilantro.

ROOT VEGETABLES

White Potato Pie

7 cups diced thin-skinned white potatoes

1 stick butter or margarine, chopped

1 medium onion, peeled and chopped

½ cup chopped fresh parsley

2 teaspoons salt

1 package frozen pie dough (not sweet) or 1 recipe Basic Pie Dough (see recipe in Chapter 11)

1 beaten egg, mixed with 1 tablespoon cold water (egg wash)

1 cup cream

1. Preheat oven to 350°F. In a large bowl, combine potatoes, butter, onion, parsley, and salt. Roll half of the pie dough ¼" thin and settle it into a 10" pie pan. Brush the rim of the crust with egg wash. Arrange the potato mixture in the crust so that it mounds slightly. Roll the top crust ¼" thin and place it onto the pie. Trim edges and crimp the pie firmly shut, using either fingers or the tines of a fork. Cut a circular vent in the center of the pie.

2. Bake 90 minutes. In a small saucepan, bring cream to a boil and add it through the vent (it may not all fit—that's okay). Bake 30 minutes more.

3. Test potatoes with a toothpick to see that they are very soft. Allow to cool about 15 minutes.

Roasted Yukon Gold Potatoes

SERVES 4

1 medium onion, peeled and roughly chopped
2 tablespoons olive oil
¼ cup chopped parsley
3 or 4 cloves garlic, peeled and minced
1½ pounds Yukon gold potatoes, washed and sliced ½" thick
1 teaspoon salt
Pepper

1. Preheat oven to 425°F. Put onion, olive oil, parsley, and garlic in blender or food processor and purée until smooth. In a large bowl, toss onion mixture with potatoes and salt, then place in a ready-made foil oven bag or a sheet of foil crimped to seal. Potatoes should be no more than two layers deep.

2. Bake on a sheet pan in center rack 45 minutes until potatoes are tender when poked with a fork. Season with pepper.

Parsnip Purée

SERVES 6

2 pounds parsnips
½ cup milk

8 tablespoons unsalted butter
Salt

1. Peel the parsnips and boil in a large pot of salted water. Cook until very tender, 10–15 minutes. Drain in a colander. While the parsnips are draining, heat the milk in a small pot.

2. Combine the parsnips and milk in a food processor or blender. With the motor going, gradually add the butter, making sure it is well mixed and the purée is very smooth. Season lightly with salt.

Turnip and Potato Gratin

▶ SERVES 8

2 tablespoons unsalted butter
2 garlic cloves, finely chopped
2½ pounds all-purpose potatoes, peeled and cut into ½" cubes
2 pounds turnips or rutabagas, peeled and cut into ½" cubes
4 cups heavy cream
2 teaspoons salt
1 teaspoon freshly ground black pepper

1. Preheat oven to 350°F. Grease the bottom and sides of a 9" square baking dish with the butter and spoon the garlic all over.

2. Arrange the potatoes and turnips in the pan. In a small saucepan, bring the cream to a boil on the stove and season with salt and pepper, then pour it over the vegetables and cover the pan with foil.

3. Bake 30 minutes, then uncover and cook another 20–25 minutes. The potatoes and turnips should be very tender and the sauce should be bubbling and browned on top when done.

Roasted Beets

▶ SERVES 8

2 pounds (about 8 tangerine-sized) beets, peeled and cut into 1" wedges
1 tablespoon olive oil
¼ teaspoon ground cinnamon
¼ teaspoon salt
Chopped fresh Italian parsley (optional)

Preheat oven to 350°F. In a large bowl, toss beets with olive oil, cinnamon, and salt. Spread into a single layer on a baking sheet (preferably nonstick). Roast on the middle rack of the oven until tender, about 1 hour, turning once after 30 minutes. If desired, serve sprinkled with chopped parsley.

Yuca con Mojo
(Yuca with Garlic and Lime)

▶ SERVES 8

1½ pounds peeled yuca, cut into 1½" chunks
½ teaspoon salt
2½ tablespoons fresh-squeezed lime juice, divided
¼ cup extra-virgin olive oil
3 large cloves garlic, peeled and finely chopped
1 tablespoon chopped fresh herb, such as cilantro or parsley (optional)

1. Add the yuca, salt, ½ teaspoon lime juice, and enough water to cover the yuca to a large pot and simmer covered about 25 minutes. It should be fork-tender but not mushy. Drain; remove woody center core. Transfer to a plate and cover to keep warm.

2. In a small skillet, heat the oil over medium heat. Remove pan from heat and add the garlic. Stir in remaining lime juice and herbs. Pour this sauce over the yuca and serve immediately.

Old-Fashioned Glazed Carrots

▶ SERVES 8

1 pound carrots, peeled and cut into 1" chunks
2 tablespoons unsalted butter
½ cup water
1½ teaspoons sugar
¼ teaspoon salt

Combine all ingredients in a heavy-bottomed skillet or pan large enough to accommodate a crowded single layer. Over medium-high heat, simmer about 5 minutes, then toss or flip the carrots. Continue cooking until the liquid is mostly evaporated and what remains is a glaze adhering to the carrots. Be careful not to go too far, or the glaze will break and become oily.

French Fries

2 pounds (about 5) high-starch potatoes, such as Russet Burbanks (Idaho baking potatoes) or Yukon golds, peeled
Peanut oil for frying
Salt

1. Cut potatoes into 2½"-long strips, ½" wide and thick; soak in a large bowl in enough cold water to cover them 30 minutes. Drain and dry with absorbent towels.

2. Heat oil to 350°F. Fry potatoes in small batches until they are soft and tender enough to mash between your fingers, about 2 minutes (make sure to allow time between each batch for the oil to come back up to temperature—a fry thermometer is essential); drain on paper towels. The potatoes may be fried again once cooled (about 5 minutes) or set aside to be refried later.

3. Heat the oil to 365°F. Fry again in small batches, stirring lightly with a tool so they don't stick together. When golden brown (2–3 minutes), remove from oil, shake off any excess, and drain on paper towels. Sprinkle immediately with salt and serve in a napkin-lined basket.

Carrot Timbales

▶ SERVES 4

1 tablespoon unsalted butter plus more as needed for ramekins

2 cups peeled, sliced carrots, cooked soft, chopped in a blender or food processor

¼ cup chopped shallots

½ teaspoon salt

Pinch of freshly grated nutmeg

Freshly ground black pepper to taste

1 cup cream or half-and-half

3 large eggs

¼ cup grated Parmesan cheese

Chopped fresh tarragon or parsley to garnish

SUBSTITUTIONS

Other vegetables may be substituted for carrots in the Carrot Timbales recipe, including cauliflower, broccoli, zucchini, or fresh sweet corn.

1. Preheat oven to 375°F. Butter four 6-ounce ramekins or custard cups. In a small skillet over medium heat, melt 1 tablespoon butter; add the carrots and cook until soft, about 3 minutes. Add the shallots to the carrots along with the salt, nutmeg, and pepper. In a small saucepan, heat the cream over medium heat until steaming but not boiling. Whisk the eggs into the vegetable mixture, then gradually whisk in the cream.

2. Divide the mixture into prepared cups and line them up in a shallow casserole or roasting pan. Add enough hot tap water to come ⅔ up the sides of the custard cups. Cover pan with foil and bake in center of oven until almost set, 25–30 minutes. Open oven door, loosen but do not remove foil, and bake 10 minutes more. Allow to rest at room temperature 10 minutes, then loosen with a knife, invert, and unmold. Garnish with chopped tarragon or parsley.

Honey-Orange Beets

▶ SERVES 4

6 medium fresh beets
1 teaspoon grated orange zest
2 tablespoons orange juice
2 teaspoons butter
1 teaspoon honey
¼ teaspoon ground ginger
Salt and freshly ground black pepper to taste

Boil beets in in a medium pot with enough water to cover 40 minutes or until tender. Drain beets and let cool slightly. Slip off skins and slice. In a medium saucepan, heat the orange zest, orange juice, butter, honey, and ginger over low heat until the butter melts. Add the beets and toss to coat. Season with salt and pepper.

Rutabaga Oven Fries

▶ SERVES 4

1 large rutabaga (wax turnip), thickly peeled
1 tablespoon olive or vegetable oil
Kosher salt
1 tablespoon finely chopped fresh thyme, rosemary, or parsley
Freshly ground black pepper

Preheat oven to 400°F. Slice rutabaga into 2½" × ½" sticks (batons); soak in cold water 30 minutes. Dry thoroughly with towels. Toss gently with oil and a light sprinkling of salt. Spread fries into a single layer on a sheet pan and bake turning occasionally until lightly browned and tender, 30–40 minutes. Remove from oven and toss with thyme, salt, and freshly ground pepper.

Herb-Mixed Turnips

▶ SERVES 4

1½ pounds turnips and rutabagas, peeled
2 tablespoons butter
1 tablespoon chopped fresh parsley
2 teaspoons chopped fresh chervil or tarragon
2 tablespoons chopped fresh chives
1 clove garlic, peeled and finely chopped
Kosher salt and freshly ground black pepper
½ cup fresh bread crumbs browned in 1 tablespoon olive oil or butter

Cook the turnips and rutabaga separately in boiling salted water until they're al dente (tender but firm—approximately 10 minutes for turnips, 20 minutes for rutabagas); drain. In a large skillet over medium heat, melt the butter. Add the turnips and rutabagas and cook over medium-high heat until golden brown. Add herbs, garlic, salt, and pepper and toss to coat. Serve topped with bread crumbs.

Slow-Cooker Rosemary Fingerling Potatoes

▶ SERVES 6

2 tablespoons extra-virgin olive oil
1½ pounds fingerling potatoes
1 teaspoon salt
¼ teaspoon freshly ground black pepper
2 tablespoons chopped fresh rosemary
1 tablespoon fresh lemon juice

TIMESAVER

To save on time when cooking potatoes, always cut them into the smallest pieces the recipe will allow and cook at the highest temperature. For this recipe, you can quarter the potatoes and cook on high heat.

1. Add the olive oil, potatoes, salt, and pepper to a 4-quart slow cooker. Cover and cook on low heat 3–4 hours.

2. Remove the cover and mix in the rosemary and lemon juice.

Celery Root, Artichoke, and Potato Gratin

▶ SERVES 8

4 tablespoons butter or olive oil
3 cloves garlic, peeled and chopped
4 large artichokes, trimmed, choke removed, cut into eighths
1 large celery root (about 1 pound), trimmed and cut into 1" cubes
8 ounces potatoes, peeled and cut into 1" cubes
1½ teaspoons kosher salt
Freshly ground black pepper
4 cups heavy cream
½ cup chopped fresh parsley

1. Preheat oven to 400°F. Butter an 11" × 13" casserole or gratin dish and sprinkle the chopped garlic evenly around, rubbing some onto the sides of the pan. Blanch the artichokes about 10 minutes in a large pot of rapidly boiling salted water, adding the celery root for the last 3 minutes. Drain well, add to casserole along with potatoes, and stir to combine. Season thoroughly with salt and pepper; add cream and parsley.

2. Place the casserole onto a sheet pan to catch any overflow. Cover with aluminum foil and bake 1 hour until cream is bubbling and potatoes are tender. Uncover and cook 15–20 minutes more until sauce is thick and starting to brown on top. Allow the casserole to rest at room temperature at least 10 minutes before serving.

Celery Root Mash

▶ SERVES 6

2 pounds celery root (sometimes called celeriac), peeled and diced into 1" pieces
1 pound white potatoes, peeled and diced into 1" pieces
½ cup milk
8 tablespoons unsalted butter
1 tablespoon snipped fresh chives (optional)
Salt

1. Boil celery root and potatoes in a large pot of lightly salted boiling water until very tender, about 20 minutes. Drain in a colander, then return to the pot and heat 30 seconds to steam out any residual water. Heat the milk and butter in a small pot.

2. Using a stiff wire whisk or potato masher, crush the vegetables until they are a soft mash. Gradually mash in the milk-butter mixture, making sure it is well mixed before adding more; fold in the chives if desired. Season lightly with salt.

Parsnip and Carrot Bake

▶ SERVES 4

1 pound carrots, peeled and cut roughly
　　into 2½" × ½" batons

8 ounces parsnips, peeled and cut
　　roughly into 2½" × ½" batons

¾ cup Vegetable Stock (see recipe in
　　Chapter 5)

2 tablespoons chopped butter

½ teaspoon salt

Chopped fresh chervil or tarragon

Freshly ground black pepper

Preheat oven to 375°F. Place carrots,
parsnips, stock, butter, and salt into
a shallow baking dish. Cover with
aluminum foil and bake until the
vegetables are soft, about 45 minutes.
Uncover and bake until vegetables brown
lightly, 10–15 minutes more. Sprinkle
with chervil and black pepper before serving.

COMMON FRESH HERBS

Most supermarkets now carry a variety of fresh herbs including thyme, chives, rosemary, sage, and oregano. But even if they don't, you can almost always find fresh Italian (flat-leaf) parsley, the best kind for cooking. Dill and cilantro are now quite common, and I recently saw fresh flash-frozen herbs in the freezer section of a store.

Carrot and Mushroom Terrine

▶ SERVES 8

¼ cup plus 1 tablespoon butter, divided

1 pound chopped mushrooms

2 cloves garlic, peeled and chopped

1 cup roughly chopped shallots

4½ cups grated carrots

5 eggs

1 cup bread crumbs

1 cup grated pecorino Romano or Parmesan cheese

Salt and freshly ground black pepper to taste

½ teaspoon dried oregano

½ teaspoon dried rosemary

1. Preheat oven to 350°F. Butter a 2-quart terrine or loaf pan. Melt ¼ cup butter in a medium heavy-bottomed skillet over medium heat. Add the mushrooms, garlic, and shallots; cook until shallots soften, about 10 minutes.

2. In a large mixing bowl, combine the shallot mixture with the carrots, eggs, half of the bread crumbs, the cheese, salt and pepper to taste, oregano, and rosemary. Pour mixture into terrine, sprinkle with remaining bread crumbs, and dot with remaining butter; cover with foil. Bake 30 minutes, then uncover and bake 5 minutes more until browned. Let stand 10 minutes before serving.

Crisp Potato Pancakes

▶ SERVES 4

1 large egg

3 large baking potatoes (such as Russet Burbank or other high-starch variety), peeled

1 medium onion, peeled

1 teaspoon salt

1 tablespoon flour

Clarified butter (ghee) or olive oil for frying

1. Beat the egg in a large bowl. Using the large-hole side of a box grater, shred the potatoes into the bowl with the egg in long motions, forming the lengthiest shreds possible. Quickly grate in the onion. Add the salt and sprinkle in the flour; toss with your hands to combine well.

2. Heat the clarified butter until it shimmers but does not smoke (a piece of potato should sizzle upon entry). Form 8 pancakes from the batter and pan-fry them in batches of 3 or 4, squeezing out excess water before gently sliding them into the pan. Cook slowly without moving them for the first 5 minutes; then loosen with a spatula. Turn after about 8 minutes when the top appears ⅓ cooked. Finish cooking on other side, about 4 minutes more. Drain on paper towels.

Rosemary New Potatoes

1 pound golf-ball-sized red-skinned new potatoes
2 tablespoons extra-virgin olive oil
3 sprigs fresh rosemary plus more for garnish
Kosher salt and freshly ground black pepper

1. Preheat oven to 375°F. Slice the potatoes into ½" thick rounds and boil them in a large pot of lightly salted water until crisp-tender, about 7 minutes. Drain well and dry very well with a towel.

2. Heat the olive oil in a large, heavy, ovensafe skillet until it shimmers but does not smoke. Add the rosemary sprigs (they should sizzle), and then slip in the potatoes. Cook without disturbing 5 minutes. Once potatoes have browned lightly on the first side, turn them over and put the pan in the oven. Cook 10 minutes. Transfer potatoes to a serving platter, season with salt and pepper, and garnish with additional rosemary sprigs.

Gingered Mashed Sweet Potatoes

SERVES 5 OR 6

4 medium sweet potatoes or yams (about 1½ pounds)
¼ cup milk
2 tablespoons butter
1 tablespoon mashed candied ginger or 1 tablespoon brown sugar plus
   ½ teaspoon ground ginger

Peel and quarter the sweet potatoes and cook in a large pot of boiling salted water until tender, about 20 minutes. Drain and return to the pan. In a small saucepan or in a bowl in the microwave, heat the milk and butter; add to the potatoes along with the candied ginger. Mash by hand or with an electric mixer. Texture will be thicker than mashed white potatoes.

Veggie-Stuffed Potatoes

▶ SERVES 4

2 large Idaho potatoes
1 tablespoon extra-virgin olive oil
½ cup chopped zucchini
½ cup mushrooms, sliced
½ cup chopped red onion
½ red pepper, chopped
1 teaspoon garlic powder
1 teaspoon all-natural sea salt
1 cup spinach, chopped
1 cup crumbled goat cheese, or vegan soft cheese

1. Preheat oven to 400°F and bake potatoes unwrapped for 30–35 minutes, or until fork-tender. Remove from heat and allow to cool for about one hour.

2. Halve potatoes and scoop out insides, leaving a thick enough skin intact to hold filling and remain sturdy, about ⅛". Return oven halves to preheated 400°F oven for 10–15 minutes to bake until golden brown.

3. While potato skins are cooking, heat the tablespoon of olive oil in a large skillet over medium heat and sauté together the zucchini, mushrooms, onion, and red pepper until all are slightly softened, about 5–7 minutes. Season with garlic powder and sea salt, and add spinach. Sauté until spinach is wilted, about 1 minute, and remove from heat.

4. Remove skins from oven, fill all four potato halves with equal amounts of the vegetable mixture, and top with equal amounts of the crumbled goat cheese.

5. Return potatoes to oven and cook until cheese is melted and lightly golden.

Twice-Baked Potatoes

▶ SERVES 4–6

4 large potatoes
2 tablespoons unsalted butter
2 tablespoons chopped onion or shallot
⅓ cup sour cream
Salt and freshly ground black pepper to taste
1 egg, beaten, divided
½ cup shredded Gruyère or Swiss cheese
About ¼ cup milk

1. Preheat oven to 450°F, then bake the potatoes 45 minutes. Remove from oven and allow to cool until they can be handled. Meanwhile, melt the butter in a small skillet over medium heat and cook the onion until softened, about 3 minutes. Halve the potatoes lengthwise and scoop out the flesh, being careful to leave a ¼"–½" shell.

2. In a large bowl, combine the potato, sour cream, onions and butter, salt and pepper, and half of the beaten egg. Mash them together thoroughly, then beat by hand or with an electric mixer, adding as much milk as necessary for a smooth consistency slightly firmer than mashed potatoes. Stir in the cheese.

3. Preheat oven to 350°F. Mound the mixture in the potato shells (for extra beauty, pipe the mixture in through a pastry bag with a wide star tip). In a small bowl, whisk the remaining egg with 1 teaspoon water and brush the tops of the stuffed potatoes with this mixture. Place potatoes on a baking sheet and bake 30 minutes until nicely browned on top and hot all the way through.

Rustic Roasted Root Vegetables

▶ SERVES 2

2 large Idaho potatoes
1 large red onion
3 large carrots, peeled
1 medium turnip
2 medium parsnips
2 cloves garlic, peeled and smashed
1 tablespoon extra-virgin olive oil
1 tablespoon Italian seasonings
1 teaspoon all-natural sea salt
1 teaspoon freshly ground black pepper
1 teaspoon ground turmeric

1. Preheat oven to 400°F and prepare a 13" × 9" baking dish with olive oil spray.

2. Cut the potatoes, onion, carrots, turnip, and parsnips into similar-sized square-inch chunks or rounds. Scatter the vegetables and smashed garlic in an even layer in the prepared dish.

3. Drizzle the vegetables with the olive oil, sprinkle with the Italian seasoning, salt and pepper, and turmeric and bake 20–25 minutes or until golden. Toss and continue to bake another 10 minutes until lightly browned and cooked through.

FOOLPROOF FARE

For even the most novice chef, potatoes and other root vegetables can make for delicious foods that are easy to prepare . . . and almost impossible to mess up. Root vegetables like potatoes, onions, carrots, garlic, turnips, and many more are a sure thing when it comes to steaming, baking, roasting, or boiling them to create a meal. Crunchy, creamy, or both, these vegetables make for foolproof fare that's not only easy but delicious and healthy, too!

Cuban Black Beans and Sweet Potatoes

▶ SERVES 4

3 cloves garlic, peeled and minced
2 large sweet potatoes, peeled and chopped small
2 tablespoons olive oil
2 (15-ounce) cans black beans, drained
¾ cup vegetable broth
1 tablespoon chili powder
1 teaspoon paprika
1 teaspoon ground cumin
1 tablespoon lime juice
Hot sauce to taste
2 cups cooked rice

1. In a large skillet or soup pot, sauté garlic and sweet potatoes in olive oil 2–3 minutes.
2. Reduce heat to medium-low and add beans, vegetable broth, chili powder, paprika, and cumin. Bring to a simmer, cover, and allow to cook 25–30 minutes until sweet potatoes are soft.
3. Stir in lime juice and hot sauce to taste. Serve hot over rice.

Gnocchi and Purple Potatoes with Broccolini

▶ SERVES 4

1 (17.6-ounce) package fresh gnocchi

1 bunch broccolini, chopped and cooked

10 baby purple potatoes, cooked and cubed

1 (13.75-ounce) can artichoke hearts, drained and quartered

3 tablespoons capers

½ cup olive oil

3 tablespoons red wine vinegar

2 tablespoons pesto

Salt and freshly ground black pepper to taste

WHAT ARE GNOCCHI?

A pasta most commonly made with mashed potatoes and flour, gnocchi, when freshly made and right from the boiling water, are so delicate they seem to whisper. Another less common version is made with semolina flour, milk, and cheese. You can make potato gnocchi yourself, but fresh ones are sold at Italian markets and some supermarkets.

1. Cook the gnocchi according to package directions, drain, and put into a serving bowl. Add the broccolini, potatoes, artichoke hearts, and capers.

2. In a small bowl, whisk together the oil, vinegar, pesto, salt, and pepper. Pour over the vegetables and toss to combine. Serve.

Swiss Chard Rolls with Root Vegetables

▶ SERVES 4

8 large leaves Swiss chard, thoroughly washed

3 tablespoons olive oil, divided

2 cups roughly chopped red onion

2 carrots, peeled and roughly chopped

2 sweet potatoes (about ½ pound), peeled and finely diced

8 cups chopped root vegetables (such as celery root, parsnips, turnips, and white potatoes, or try Latino roots such as yuca, cassava, and taro)

¼ cup roughly chopped fresh Italian parsley

Juice of 2 limes (about 4 tablespoons)

2 teaspoons chopped fresh cilantro (optional)

Kosher salt and freshly ground black pepper

1 cup stock or water

1. Remove the stems from the chard; chop the stems finely and reserve the leaves. Heat 2 tablespoons of the olive oil over medium heat in a heavy-bottomed Dutch oven or large skillet. Add the chard stems, red onion, carrots, sweet potatoes, root vegetables, parsley, lime juice, and cilantro; season well with salt and pepper.

2. Bring a large pot of salted water to a boil. Blanch the chard leaves 3–4 minutes, then drain and cool. Spoon ¼ cup of filling onto the stem end of a chard leaf. Fold in the sides to envelop the filling; roll away from yourself, keeping even tension so the rolls remain plump. Add the remaining 1 tablespoon oil to a large skillet and line the rolls up in the skillet; add 1 cup water or stock and season lightly with salt. Cook 10 minutes; serve garnished with remaining filling.

Fiery Indian Potatoes

6 large potatoes, peeled and cubed

3 tablespoons vegetable oil, or more as needed

5 dried red chilies, crushed

1 tablespoon mustard seeds

1 teaspoon ground turmeric

1 teaspoon red chili powder

Salt and freshly ground black pepper to taste

1 tablespoon ground coriander

1 cup chopped fresh cilantro

1. Steam the potato cubes until just tender. Set aside.

2. Heat the oil over medium heat in a large skillet or wok and sauté the potatoes 2 minutes. Add the chilies, mustard seeds, turmeric, chili powder, salt, and pepper and continue cooking over medium heat, stirring until the seasonings are well mixed and the potatoes begin to brown.

3. Stir in the coriander, garnish with the cilantro, and serve.

Chipotle and Thyme Sweet Potatoes

SERVES 6

6 cups cubed sweet potatoes

4 tablespoons butter or vegan margarine

3 cloves garlic, peeled and minced

1 teaspoon dried chipotle pepper

½ teaspoon dried thyme

1 teaspoon salt

¼ teaspoon freshly ground black pepper

Add all ingredients to a 4-quart slow cooker. Cover and cook on medium heat 4 hours.

Overly Stuffed Baked Sweet Potato

▶ SERVES 1

1 large sweet potato
½ cup mild or hot salsa
¾ cup grated Cheddar cheese
1 medium jalapeño pepper, seeded and diced
½ cup cubed Monterey jack cheese
1 cup vegetarian chili
Chopped fresh cilantro for garnish

1. Bake the sweet potato in a 350°F oven until tender, 50–60 minutes. Remove from the oven and, when it is cool enough to handle, slit open the top and scoop out the flesh, leaving a thin layer of flesh around the interior.

2. In a medium bowl, mix the sweet potato flesh with the salsa, grated Cheddar, and jalapeño. Spoon it back into the skin and dot the top with the Monterey jack. Return the sweet potato to the oven to cook until the cheese melts.

3. Meanwhile, heat the chili in a small saucepan over medium heat; when the cheese has melted on top of the sweet potato, put the sweet potato on a serving plate and spoon the chili over top. Garnish with the cilantro and enjoy.

Roasted Garlic Mashed Potatoes

▶ SERVES 6

3 heads garlic
2 pounds red bliss potatoes, peeled and cut into large chunks
8 tablespoons butter
½ cup milk or cream
1½ teaspoons salt
Ground white pepper to taste

1. Preheat oven to 350°F. Wrap all three garlic heads into a pouch fashioned from aluminum foil and place in the center of the oven. Roast until garlic is very soft and yields to gentle finger pressure, about 1 hour and 15 minutes. Cut the garlic bulbs in half laterally. Using your hands, squeeze out the roasted garlic and push it through a sieve.

2. Boil potatoes in a large pot with enough lightly salted water to cover until very tender, 25–30 minutes depending on type and size of potato pieces. Drain the potatoes well, then return them to the pot, put them on the stove, and cook over moderate heat 30–60 seconds to steam off any excess moisture.

3. Heat the butter and milk together in a small saucepan over medium heat until the butter melts.

4. For smoothest mashed potatoes, force the potatoes through a ricer. Otherwise, mash them in a large bowl with a potato masher or stiff wire whisk. Add the roasted garlic purée, salt, pepper, and the milk mixture to the potatoes and mix just enough to incorporate. Serve immediately or keep warm for later service in a double boiler.

LEAFY GREENS AND CRUCIFEROUS VEGETABLES

Spinach and Tomato Sauté

▶ SERVES 4

3 teaspoons butter, divided

6 plum tomatoes, roughly chopped

1 teaspoon ground coriander

2 bunches flat-leaf spinach, washed very thoroughly

½ teaspoon salt

Freshly ground black pepper

In a large skillet or heavy-bottomed Dutch oven, melt 2 teaspoons butter over medium-high heat. Add the tomatoes and coriander; cook until softened, about 5 minutes. Add the spinach in handfuls, allowing each handful to wilt before adding the next. Season it well with salt and pepper. Finish by swirling in the remaining butter.

NONREACTIVE POTS: WELCOME TO THE STEEL AND GLASS GENERATION

Aluminum and copper, commonly used materials in pots and pans, react with (and alter the flavor and color of) acidic foods. Always use pans with a stainless steel or glass cooking surface to avoid sour tomato sauce, discolored green beans, and "off"-tasting soups. For the lightweight and even heat of aluminum and copper, combined with the nonreactive property of steel, buy aluminum or copper alloy pots clad to a steel "jacket" (inner lining).

Aloo Gobi (Cauliflower and Potato Curry)

▶ SERVES 8

3 tablespoons vegetable oil

2 large onions, peeled and finely chopped (about 5 cups)

4 medium jalapeño or other chili peppers, seeded and finely chopped

1 (1") piece fresh ginger, peeled and finely chopped

3 medium tomatoes, finely chopped

1¼ teaspoons chili powder

1 teaspoon ground turmeric

1 teaspoon ground coriander

2 teaspoons kosher salt

2 pounds potatoes, peeled and cut into large chunks

1 large head cauliflower, cut into large chunks

1 teaspoon garam masala (spice mixture available at specialty stores—or make your own by combining 1 teaspoon each of ground cardamom, cumin seed, cloves, black pepper, and ground cinnamon)

Chopped fresh cilantro or parsley for garnish

1. Heat the oil in a heavy skillet over medium-high heat and cook the onions, jalapeño, and ginger until brown, about 10 minutes. Add the tomatoes, chili powder, turmeric, coriander, and salt; cook 5 minutes more until spices are fragrant and evenly dispersed. Mix in the potatoes and cauliflower plus enough water to come halfway up the vegetables.

2. Cover the pan and simmer 20 minutes, stirring occasionally until the potatoes and cauliflower are very tender. Add the garam masala powder; cook 5 minutes more. Serve garnished with cilantro.

Stir-Fried Asian Greens

▶ SERVES 8

1 bunch (about 1 pound) collard greens, thinly sliced

1 small head (about 1 pound) Chinese cabbage (barrel-shaped napa cabbage), thinly sliced

1 bunch watercress, stem ends trimmed

2 tablespoons peanut oil

1 (10-ounce) package white or cremini mushrooms

1 large "horse" carrot or 2 cello carrots, peeled, sliced thinly on the bias (diagonal)

¼ pound snow peas, halved diagonally

1 medium red onion, peeled, halved, and sliced with the grain

2" piece fresh ginger, peeled and julienned

3 cloves garlic, finely chopped

Salt and white pepper to taste

2 tablespoons soy sauce

1 teaspoon sesame oil

Black sesame seeds or toasted white sesame seeds for garnish (optional)

Mix together the collards, cabbage, and watercress in a large colander; wash thoroughly, drain, and dry. Heat the peanut oil in a large skillet (13") over high heat until it is shimmery but not smoky. Add the mushrooms, carrots, snow peas, onion, ginger, and garlic; sauté 2 minutes, stirring frequently, allowing some parts to brown. Season it well with salt and white pepper. Add the greens, soy sauce, and sesame oil. Toss or stir; cook only 1 minute until the greens begin to wilt. Serve immediately with a sprinkling of sesame seeds.

Shanghai Bok Choy with Garlic and Black Bean Sauce

▶ SERVES 4

8 heads Shanghai (baby) bok choy

2 cups Mushroom Vegetable Stock (see recipe in Chapter 5) or other strong vegetable stock

1 teaspoon sugar

1 tablespoon Chinese fermented black bean sauce or 1 teaspoon Chinese fermented black beans (both available from Asian specialty stores)

2 teaspoons hoisin sauce (available in the Asian section of most supermarkets)

2 teaspoons cornstarch dissolved in ¼ cup cold water

2 teaspoons peanut or other oil

2 teaspoons (about 3 cloves) chopped garlic

Salt to taste

Dash of Asian hot chili paste (optional)

1. Halve the bok choy heads lengthwise and blanch in a large pot of rapidly boiling salted water 3–4 minutes until crisp-tender. Drain and plunge immediately into a large bowl of ice water to stop the cooking. In a medium saucepan, bring the stock to a boil. Whisk in sugar, bean sauce or beans, and hoisin. Simmer 10 minutes, then whisk in cornstarch slurry to thicken; cook 5 minutes more covered. It should have the consistency of honey. Taste for seasoning.

2. Heat the oil in a large skillet over medium heat. Add garlic and allow it to sizzle until it begins to turn golden brown. Immediately add the blanched bok choy, season lightly with salt, and cook until vegetable is warmed through. Add chili paste if desired. Transfer to a serving platter and spoon on the black bean sauce, reserving any extra to be served on the side at the table.

Gai Lan (Chinese Broccoli) with Toasted Garlic

▶ SERVES 4

1 pound gai lan (Chinese broccoli) or other type of broccoli
2 tablespoons peanut oil
5 cloves garlic, peeled and finely chopped
Pinch of crushed red pepper (optional)
Kosher salt and freshly ground black pepper
Lemon wedges

1. Prepare a deep bowl full of salted ice water; set aside. Bring a large pot of salted water (it should be as salty as tears) to a rapid, rolling boil. Trim any frayed ends from the stems of the gai lan. Cook it by handfuls in the boiling water only until crisp-tender, about 4–5 minutes; plunge immediately into the ice bath. Drain.

2. In a large skillet or wok, heat the oil over medium heat until it is hot. Add the garlic and red pepper (if using) and cook without stirring until the garlic begins to turn golden brown. Immediately add the blanched gai lan and toss gently to stop the garlic from browning further. Cook until the gai lan is thoroughly hot. Season well with salt and pepper. Serve with lemon wedges.

Braised Swiss Chard

▶ SERVES 4

1 large bunch (about 1½ pounds) red or green Swiss chard
1 cup Mushroom Vegetable Stock (see recipe in Chapter 5) or liquid from cooking beans
Salt and freshly ground black pepper to taste
1 tablespoon olive oil
2 medium shallots, peeled and finely chopped (about ¼ cup)
1 tablespoon unsalted butter
Lemon wedges

1. Wash the chard thoroughly under running water and shake dry. Using your hands, tear the leafy parts away from the stems; set aside. Cut the stems into bite-sized pieces. In a nonreactive skillet (see the Nonreactive Pots: Welcome to the Steel and Glass Generation sidebar in this chapter), bring the stock to a boil; add the stem pieces. Season with salt and pepper; cook until tender. Transfer them to a bowl or plate, reserving their cooking liquid. Wipe out the skillet.

2. Return the skillet to the heat and add the olive oil and shallots. Cook 1 minute until they sizzle and soften slightly. Add the chard leaves and cook only until they wilt, about 2–3 minutes. Add back the stems plus 2 tablespoons of their cooking liquid. Bring to a simmer and swirl in the butter. Taste for seasoning. Serve with lemon wedges.

Cabbage Stewed in Tomato Sauce

▶ SERVES 8

2 tablespoons olive oil
1 medium onion, peeled and roughly chopped
1 small head (about 2 pounds) green or red cabbage
1 teaspoon caraway seeds
Salt and freshly ground black pepper
2 cups tomato sauce
2 teaspoons brown sugar

Heat the oil in a large Dutch oven. Add the onions and cook until they are translucent, about 5 minutes. Add the cabbage, caraway seeds, and a little salt and pepper; cook over medium heat until soft and saucy, about 5 minutes more. Stir in tomato sauce and brown sugar. Lower heat to a simmer and cook covered 1 hour, stirring occasionally until the cabbage is very tender and has taken on color from the sauce.

Basic Buttered Brussels Sprouts

▶ SERVES 4

1 pint Brussels sprouts
2 ounces (½ stick) unsalted butter

Salt and white pepper
Pinch of nutmeg (optional)

1. Remove outer leaves from sprouts and trim the stems so that they're flush with the sprout bottoms. Halve the sprouts by cutting through the stem end.

2. Boil in small batches in a large pot in 4 quarts of well-salted, rapidly boiling water, about 2–3 minutes. Drain.

3. In a medium (10") sauté pan over medium heat, melt the butter and add the cooked sprouts; toss with the seasonings to coat. Serve with lemon wedges.

Spinach with Pine Nuts (Pignoli) and Garlic

▶ SERVES 4

¼ cup pine nuts (pignoli)

3 tablespoons extra-virgin olive oil

2 cloves garlic, finely chopped

2 pounds washed spinach leaves, stems removed

Salt and freshly ground black pepper

Lemon wedges

1. Gently toast the nuts in a dry sauté pan over medium heat until they start to brown. Set aside. In a very large pan, heat the olive oil and garlic over medium heat until it sizzles and starts to brown.

2. Add ⅓ of the spinach and the pine nuts and sauté until spinach is wilted and lets off some liquid, about 2–3 minutes. Add the rest of the spinach in batches, seasoning with salt and pepper as it cooks. Serve with lemon wedges.

THE INCREDIBLE SHRINKING SPINACH!

Leafy green vegetables look huge when they're taking up cubic yards of refrigerator space, but seem to shrivel into mouse-sized portions when you cook them. They shrink to one-sixth their raw volume upon cooking. Stem trimmage also means they're less voluminous than you'd think. Figure on a half pound of raw greens per person (slightly less if the stems are eaten, as with Swiss chard).

Smoky Spiced Collard Greens with Turnip

▶ SERVES 4

1 bunch collard or turnip greens

1 medium white turnip, peeled and diced into ¼" pieces

1 medium onion, peeled and chopped

1 chipotle chili, dried or canned, cut in half

1 tablespoon olive oil

1 teaspoon salt

1 cup Vegetable Stock (see recipe in Chapter 5)

1. Wash greens and remove the stems. Cut leaves into long thin strips (julienne).

2. In a large heavy-bottomed pot, sauté the turnip, onion, and chili in olive oil until the onion is translucent. Add the greens and salt and sauté a few minutes more until greens are wilted.

3. Add stock or water, bring to a boil, and reduce heat to simmer 20 minutes or until greens are very tender and turnips are soft.

Collard Greens with Tomatoes and Cheddar

▶ SERVES 4

2 pounds collard greens, stems and ribs removed

2 tablespoons olive oil

1 tablespoon finely chopped garlic (about 2 cloves)

4 ripe medium red or yellow tomatoes (or a combination)

1 teaspoon salt

1 teaspoon dried oregano

4 ounces shredded Cheddar cheese

Bring a large pot of salted water to a rolling boil. Cook the greens until tender, about 10 minutes; drain and roughly chop. Heat the oil in a large heavy-bottomed skillet over medium-high heat. Add the garlic; allow it to sizzle 30 seconds before adding the collards, tomatoes, salt, and oregano. Cook 4 minutes just until the tomatoes are hot. Serve topped with the shredded cheese.

Broccoli Florets with Lemon Butter Sauce

▶ SERVES 4

2 small shallots, peeled and finely chopped
¼ cup white cooking wine
Juice of 1 lemon, divided
8 ounces cold unsalted butter, cut into small pieces
Salt and white pepper
1 large head broccoli, broken into florets

1. Place the shallots, wine, and half of the lemon juice in a small saucepan over medium heat. Simmer until almost dry. Reduce heat to very low and stir in a few small pieces of butter, swirling it in with a wire whisk until it is mostly melted. Gradually add the remaining butter whisking constantly until all is used and sauce is smooth. Never boil. Season the sauce with salt, white pepper, and remaining lemon juice to taste. Keep in a warm place, but not over heat.

2. Wash the broccoli and boil in a large pot with 4 quarts rapidly boiling, salted water 4–5 minutes. Drain and serve with lemon butter sauce.

ANTIOXIDANTS

Antioxidants are vitamins and other substances that help your body expel free radicals, harmful by-products of cellular oxygen use. Antioxidants are believed to have cancer-fighting properties, aid in heart regulation, and strengthen immune systems. Dark, leafy greens are high in antioxidants such as beta carotene (which your body turns into vitamin A), selenium, and vitamins C and E. Scientists are still unsure exactly which antioxidants work on which parts of the body, so a balanced diet is still the best diet.

Stuffed Cabbage

▶ SERVES 6

1 head (about 1½ pounds) green
   cabbage, stem core cut out
2 tablespoons olive oil
1 large onion, peeled and roughly
   chopped
1 bunch scallions, chopped
1 bunch basil, leaves picked, washed
   well, and cut into julienne
½ cup chopped fresh Italian parsley
1 teaspoon dried oregano
½ teaspoon dried thyme
Kosher salt and freshly ground black
   pepper
1 cup cooked barley, spelt, brown rice,
   or other whole grain
¼ cup puréed silken tofu
¼ cup Vegetable Stock (see recipe in
   Chapter 5)
2 cups tomato sauce

WHERE VEGETARIANS SHOP

Seek out your nearest natural foods and/or gourmet specialty food shop. That's where you'll find the delectable grains, spices, chilies, and whole foods essential to a healthy vegetarian life. Mainstream supermarkets carry most or all of what you'll see in this book, but you'll be surprised at the difference in quality (and sometimes, believe it or not, lower prices) you'll find at these stores.

1. Preheat oven to 350°F. Bring a large stockpot of water to a boil; submerge the cabbage in it and cook about 5 minutes. Peel off the first few softened leaves, then put the cabbage back in to soften some more. Repeat this process until you have 12 softened leaves; cut the thick vein from their stem ends. Finely shred the remaining cabbage.

2. Heat the olive oil in a large skillet over high heat 1 minute; add the chopped cabbage, onions, scallions, basil, parsley, oregano, and thyme. Season thoroughly with salt and pepper. Cover and cook until vegetables are tender, about 15 minutes, stirring occasionally; drain. In a large bowl, add cabbage mixture, cooked barley, and puréed tofu and mix to combine. Taste for seasoning and add more salt if necessary—it should be highly seasoned.

3. Place the softened cabbage leaves on a work surface with the stem end closest to you. Distribute the filling onto the leaves, placing it closest to the stem end. Fold the sides in to envelop the filling, then roll away from yourself, keeping even tension to keep the rolls plump. Place the rolls in a baking dish, add the vegetable stock, and bake 30 minutes. Make small pools of tomato sauce on six plates and serve two rolls atop the sauce for each portion.

Braised Red Cabbage
(Chou Rouge à la Flamande)

▶ SERVES 8

1 small head (about 2 pounds) red cabbage

1 teaspoon salt

Pinch of grated nutmeg

1 tablespoon oil

1 tablespoon red wine vinegar

4 medium Granny Smith (Pippin) apples, peeled, cored, and cut into ¼" slices

1 tablespoon brown sugar

Preheat oven to 325°F (if using). Wash cabbage and discard tough outer leaves; quarter, core, and thinly slice (julienne) it. Sprinkle shredded cabbage with salt and nutmeg. Heat oil over medium heat in a large Dutch oven or ovenproof casserole dish with a tight-fitting lid; add cabbage and red vinegar. Cover and cook over low heat at least 1 hour either on the stovetop or in oven. Add the apples and sugar; cook another 30 minutes until cabbage is very tender and apples are mostly dissolved.

Spinach-Stuffed Vegetables

▶ SERVES 4

1 tablespoon olive oil
1 tablespoon whole coriander seeds
3 medium shallots, peeled and roughly chopped
¼ teaspoon crushed red pepper (optional)
2 pounds spinach, washed and stemmed
½ teaspoon salt plus more to taste
¼ cup crumbled feta cheese (optional)
4 plum tomatoes, tops cut off and insides scooped out
1 medium zucchini, cut into 4 (2") cylinders
1 medium yellow squash, cut into 4 (2") cylinders
4 large stuffing mushrooms, stems removed
White pepper to taste
Lemon wedges

1. Heat the olive oil and coriander seeds in a small pan over medium heat until very hot but not smoking—the coriander seeds should become fragrant but not brown. Strain the oil into a large skillet or Dutch oven; discard the seeds. Add the shallots and crushed pepper if using to the skillet and cook over medium heat 1 minute—they should sizzle but not brown. Add the spinach all at once; season with salt and cook, stirring, just until spinach is wilted, about 2–3 minutes. Transfer to a colander to cool.

2. Chop the spinach roughly on a cutting board and combine with the feta cheese if using in a medium bowl. Trim the bottoms of the tomatoes just enough to help them stand straight. Using a small spoon or melon baller, scoop enough of the seeded center from the zucchini and yellow squash to form a teaspoon-sized pocket. Season all the vegetables liberally with salt and white pepper. Spoon the spinach mixture into tomatoes, zucchini, squash, and mushrooms, mounding slightly on top. Any extra spinach may be used to line the plates when serving.

3. Arrange the vegetables in a steamer basket. Steam over rapidly boiling water just until the zucchini becomes tender, about 6 minutes. Serve hot or at room temperature along with remaining spinach filling and lemon wedges.

Kale with Tuscan White Beans and Thyme

▶ SERVES 4

2 pounds kale, stems and ribs removed
1 tablespoon olive oil
1 medium red onion, peeled chopped
1 tablespoon chopped garlic
Pinch of crushed red pepper
2 teaspoons chopped fresh thyme or ½ teaspoon dried
¼ cup dry sherry or white wine
2 (15.5-ounce) cans cannellini beans, rinsed and drained
Salt and freshly ground black pepper
Grated vegan Parmesan cheese (optional)

1. Bring a large pot of well-salted water to a rolling boil. Add the kale and cook 10 minutes until it has lost its waxy coating and the leaves are tender. Transfer to a colander to drain, reserving about ½ cup of the cooking liquid. Roughly chop the kale.

2. Heat the oil in a large skillet or Dutch oven. Add the onion, garlic, red pepper, and thyme. Cook over medium heat until the onions are soft and starting to brown around the edges. Splash in the sherry; cook 5 minutes until all alcohol has evaporated. Add back the kale and the beans; cook 10 minutes more until the kale and beans are heated through. Season with salt and pepper. Serve sprinkled with grated Parmesan cheese if desired.

Creamed Spinach

SERVES 4

2 pounds spinach, stemmed and washed
½ cup heavy cream
½ teaspoon salt
Grated nutmeg
Freshly ground black pepper

1. Heat a large nonreactive skillet or Dutch oven over medium heat and cook the spinach with a few drops of water until just wilted, about 2–3 minutes. Drain, rinse, and squeeze dry in a colander. Chop the spinach finely.

2. In a medium skillet, bring the cream to a boil; add the salt, nutmeg, and pepper. Stir in the spinach; cook until most of the water has cooked out and the spinach is thick. If desired, purée in a blender or food processor.

Grilled Radicchio

SERVES 4

4 heads radicchio
1 tablespoon extra-virgin olive oil
1 lemon, halved, plus lemon wedges for garnish
Salt and freshly ground black pepper to taste

1. Quarter the radicchio heads through the root end. In a mixing bowl, drizzle the olive oil over the radicchio, squeeze on the lemon juice, and season with salt and pepper; toss to coat.

2. Heat a grill or stovetop grill pan to medium heat. Lay the radicchio cut-side down across the grill ribs. Cook until wilting is visible from the sides, only about 2 minutes. Turn to the other cut side and cook 1–2 minutes more, pulling it from the grill before it goes completely limp. Serve with extra lemon wedges on the side.

Kale with Garlic and Thyme

▶ SERVES 4

2 pounds kale, stems and ribs removed
1 tablespoon olive oil
1 medium red onion, peeled and chopped
1 tablespoon chopped garlic
Pinch of crushed red pepper
2 teaspoons chopped fresh thyme leaves or ½ teaspoon dried
¼ cup dry sherry or white wine
Salt and freshly ground black pepper to taste

1. Bring a large pot of well-salted water to a rolling boil. Add the kale and cook 10 minutes until it has lost its waxy coating and the leaves are tender. Transfer to a colander to drain, reserving about ½ cup of the cooking liquid. Roughly chop the kale.

2. Heat the oil in a large skillet or Dutch oven. Add the onion, garlic, red pepper, and thyme. Cook over medium heat until the onions are soft and starting to brown around the edges.

3. Splash in the sherry; cook 5 minutes until all alcohol has evaporated. Add back the kale; cook 10 minutes more. Season with salt and pepper.

Garlicky Broccoli Raab

▶ SERVES 4

1 pound broccoli raab, bottoms trimmed
2 tablespoons good-quality olive oil
2 tablespoons finely chopped garlic
Pinch of crushed red pepper (optional)
Salt and freshly ground black pepper
Lemon wedges

Bring a large pot of salted water to a rolling boil. Add the raab and cook until tender but still firm, about 5 minutes; shock in a bowl of ice water and drain. Heat the olive oil in a large heavy-bottomed skillet over medium heat 1 minute. Add the garlic and red pepper if using and cook stirring with a wooden spoon until garlic is golden. Add all of the raab at once; toss to coat. Season well with salt and pepper (make sure to taste as you season, remembering that the raab should have been blanched and shocked in salted water!). When the vegetable is hot, serve with lemon wedges on the side.

Spinach and Feta Pie

▶ SERVES 8

1 bunch fresh spinach (about 4 cups)

3 tablespoons olive oil

1 medium yellow onion, peeled and chopped

1 cup grated Swiss cheese

2 large eggs

1¼ cups light cream

½ teaspoon salt

¼ teaspoon freshly ground black pepper

Pinch of ground nutmeg

¼ cup grated vegan Parmesan cheese

1 (10") deep-dish pie crust, prebaked 5 minutes at 375°F

6 ounces crumbled feta cheese

2 medium tomatoes, sliced (optional)

1. Preheat oven to 350°F. Wash and stem the spinach; add spinach and a few drops of water to a large skillet over medium heat and steam until wilted, about 2–3 minutes. Squeeze out excess water and chop. Heat the olive oil in a small skillet and cook the onion until golden, about 7 minutes; toss with the spinach. Stir in the Swiss cheese.

2. Combine the eggs, cream, salt, pepper, nutmeg, and Parmesan cheese in a blender. Blend 1 minute. Spread the spinach mixture into the crust. Top with feta cheese and decorate with tomatoes if desired. Pour on the egg mixture, pressing through with your fingers to make sure it soaks through to the crust. Bake 45 minutes until a knife inserted in the pie comes out clean. Serve hot or room temperature.

Szechuan Stir-Fried Cabbage with Hot Peppers

▶ SERVES 4–6

¼ cup plus 2 tablespoons peanut or other neutral oil, divided

8 dried red chili peppers, quartered and seeded

1 (1") piece fresh ginger, peeled and finely chopped

1 medium head cabbage (preferably Chinese cabbage, but any variety is okay), washed and chopped into 2" pieces

½ teaspoon cornstarch

1 tablespoon soy sauce

1 teaspoon sugar

1 teaspoon rice wine vinegar

1 teaspoon Asian sesame oil

1. Heat ¼ cup of the oil in a wok or skillet over high heat. Stir in the peppers and fry, stirring, 1 minute until the peppers darken in color. Transfer the peppers and oil to a bowl and set aside.

2. Pour remaining 2 tablespoons of oil into the wok; add the ginger and cook a few seconds until fragrant. Add the cabbage all at once. Fry, stirring, 1 minute. Combine the cornstarch and soy sauce together in a small bowl. Add to the wok. Stir until the cornstarch cooks and forms a thick sauce; add the sugar and vinegar. Sprinkle in the sesame oil and pour in the red peppers and their oil. Stir to combine well. Transfer to a serving bowl.

Spinach Pancakes with Cardamom

▶ SERVES 4

1 tablespoon olive oil
2 teaspoons finely chopped garlic
2 pounds fresh spinach, washed and stemmed
4 cracked-open cardamom pods or ½ teaspoon ground
1 teaspoon salt
Freshly ground black pepper
2 ounces egg substitute
1 cup plus 2 tablespoons bread crumbs, divided
Oil for frying
Lemon wedges

1. Heat the olive oil in a large skillet or Dutch oven over high heat; add the garlic. Cook 30 seconds until garlic becomes clear and fragrant; add the spinach, cardamom pods, salt, and pepper to taste. Cook just until spinach is wilted, about 2–3 minutes; transfer to a colander to cool.

2. Squeeze all excess water from spinach. Combine with egg substitute and 2 tablespoons bread crumbs; mix well. Form into four pancakes; dredge in remaining bread crumbs. Heat fry oil in a heavy-bottomed skillet and fry cakes until browned on both sides and hot in the center. Serve with lemon wedges.

Baked Spinach Tart

2 large eggs

1 cup plain nonfat or whole-milk yogurt

1 cup feta cheese

1 cup shredded mozzarella cheese

1 bunch fresh spinach, preferably organic, well rinsed, wilted, and chopped

½ cup chopped onion

Salt and freshly ground black pepper to taste

1 (9") unbaked deep-dish pie shell

½ pint grape tomatoes

1. Preheat oven to 350°F.

2. In a medium bowl, beat the eggs until foamy. Stir in the yogurt, feta cheese, mozzarella cheese, spinach, and onions; mix well until combined. Season with salt and pepper.

3. Spoon the mixture into the pie shell and push the tomatoes into the top of the mixture.

4. Bake about 40 minutes or until the mixture is firm to the touch. Let it cool slightly before slicing and serving.

TOMATOES AND OTHER VEGETABLES

Cumin-Roasted Butternut Squash

▶ SERVES 8

1 medium butternut squash (2–3 pounds)
2 tablespoons ground cumin
2 tablespoons olive oil
Salt and coarsely ground black pepper
1 tablespoon roughly chopped fresh Italian (flat-leaf) parsley

1. Preheat oven to 375°F. Cut the squash in two crosswise just above the bulbous bottom. Place the cut side of the cylindrical barrel down on a cutting board and peel it with a knife or potato peeler, removing all rind. Repeat with the bottom part, then cut bottom in half and remove seeds.

2. Dice squash into 1" chunks. In a large mixing bowl, toss squash with cumin, oil, salt, and pepper.

3. Spread into a single layer on a doubled baking sheet and roast 25 minutes; turn squash and roast an additional 15 minutes until browned and tender. Serve sprinkled with chopped parsley.

Herbed Red and Yellow Tomatoes on Honey-Nut Bread

▶ SERVES 4

¼ cup extra-virgin olive oil

¼ cup balsamic vinegar

1 tablespoon Dijon mustard

½ bunch fresh oregano or marjoram, roughly chopped

½ bunch fresh Italian parsley, roughly chopped

1 small bunch fresh chives, chopped

2 ripe beefsteak or other sweet variety red tomatoes, sliced ½" thick

2 yellow acid-free tomatoes, sliced ½" thick

8 slices honey-nut bread or other type sweet-dough bread containing whole grains, sliced ½" thick

Coarse salt and freshly ground black pepper to taste

1. Whisk together oil, vinegar, and mustard in a small steel bowl. Fold in chopped herbs.

2. Lay tomato slices in a single layer into a glass (nonreactive) dish and pour most of the dressing over them, reserving about 2 tablespoons. Allow to marinate at room temperature about 10 minutes.

3. Toast the whole-grain bread and drizzle with remaining dressing. Shingle tomatoes in alternating colors. Season with coarse salt and freshly ground black pepper.

Mushroom-Stuffed Tomatoes

▶ SERVES 6 AS AN APPETIZER OR SIDE DISH OR UP TO 12 AS A
TASTY GARNISH

4 medium shallots, peeled and chopped fine
2 tablespoons olive oil, divided
1 pound white mushrooms, washed and chopped fine
1 teaspoon salt plus 2 pinches, divided
¼ cup finely chopped fresh parsley
Freshly ground black pepper
6 large ripe plum tomatoes, halved crosswise and bottoms trimmed flat
3 tablespoons bread crumbs

1. Preheat oven to 350°F. Sauté chopped shallots with 1 tablespoon olive
   oil in a large skillet over medium heat. Add chopped mushrooms (if
   some don't fit, you can add them later when the rest have wilted down)
   and 1 teaspoon salt and raise heat to high. Cook, stirring occasionally,
   until mushrooms have given up their water and most of it has
   evaporated.

2. Stir in chopped parsley, remove from heat, and season with freshly
   ground black pepper.

3. Scoop the innards from the tomatoes and season the tomato cups
   with 2 pinches salt. Fill each tomato with mushroom filling so that it
   mounds slightly; top each with a sprinkle of bread crumbs. Line into
   a baking dish and drizzle with remaining olive oil. Bake 25 minutes
   until soft.

Fried Green Tomatoes with Remoulade Sauce

1 cup mayonnaise (preferably homemade)

1 hard-boiled egg, finely chopped

1 tablespoon chopped capers

1 tablespoon chopped cornichons or dill pickle

1 teaspoon chopped fresh parsley

Dash of hot pepper sauce or pinch of cayenne pepper

3 large green tomatoes, sliced ½" thick (should total 12–14 slices)

Flour for dredging

6 large beaten eggs mixed with ½ cup milk

4 cups plain or seasoned bread crumbs (preferably homemade)

3 cups light oil, such as canola or peanut, for frying

1. Make the Remoulade Sauce: In a small bowl, combine mayonnaise with chopped egg, capers, pickle, parsley, and hot sauce. Taste for seasoning and refrigerate.

2. Dredge each tomato slice in flour, then eggs, then bread crumbs, pressing the bread crumbs to ensure adherence. Fry in small batches over medium-low heat (325°F oil temperature) until they feel tender when tested with a fork. Season with salt and serve immediately with Remoulade Sauce.

Tomato Confit with Fine Herbs

5 large ripe but firm beefsteak tomatoes, cored, halved crosswise, and
   seeded

12 big sprigs assorted fresh herbs like thyme, oregano, rosemary,
   parsley, etc.

3 tablespoons olive oil

1 teaspoon salt

1. Preheat oven to 275°F. In a large bowl, toss the tomatoes gently with
   the herbs, olive oil, and salt; then arrange cut-side down in a baking
   dish so that the herbs are under and touching them.

2. Bake 2 hours until flesh is very soft to the touch and skin looks
   wrinkled.

3. Cool until you can touch them and carefully remove the skins. Serve
   warm.

Red and Yellow Plum Tomato Chutney

▶ YIELDS ABOUT 3 CUPS

⅓ cup sugar
½ cup water
Juice of 1 lemon
6 ripe red plum tomatoes, seeded and roughly chopped
6 ripe yellow plum tomatoes, seeded and roughly chopped
¼ cup finely diced red onion
¼ cup roughly chopped fresh cilantro (optional)

Mix sugar with ½ cup water in a medium saucepan. Cook over high heat until water is evaporated and molten sugar begins to turn golden brown. Pour in lemon juice to stop the sugar from cooking and bring it up from the bottom of the pan. Add the chopped tomatoes and red onion. Simmer no more than 5 minutes (this is to warm the tomatoes, not cook them). Remove from heat. Allow to cool in a colander, letting the excess water released from the warmed tomatoes drain out. Stir in chopped cilantro.

New Mexico Chili Sauce

▶ MAKES 3 CUPS

1 teaspoon olive oil

1 medium onion, peeled and roughly chopped

5 New Mexico chilies, seeded, soaked, and puréed

1 (28-ounce) jar roasted-garlic-flavored marinara sauce

½ teaspoon ground cumin

½ teaspoon dried oregano

Heat the oil in a saucepan over medium heat. Add onion; cook, stirring occasionally, until translucent, about 5 minutes. Add chili purée; cook 3 minutes more. Add the marinara sauce, cumin, and oregano. Simmer 10 minutes. Purée in a blender until very smooth.

IT'S NOT HOT, IT'S CHILI

Fruity, smoky, citrusy, woodsy . . . These are just a few words to describe the flavors of various chilies. Make dried chilies ready for use by toasting them in a 350°F oven for 5 minutes, until they soften, become fragrant, and smoke lightly. Then soak them in enough water to cover for 1 hour and purée in a blender with just enough soaking liquid to make a thick purée circulate in the blender vase. For less heat, remove the seeds before soaking.

Chilaquiles (Tortilla Stew)

▶ SERVES 2

4 cups tortilla chips (any color)
2 cups Vegetable Stock (see recipe in Chapter 5)
1 cup spicy tomato sauce
4 large eggs (optional)
2 tablespoons sour cream or tofu sour cream
Chopped fresh cilantro

Place the chips in a large skillet over high heat. Add 1 cup vegetable stock and the tomato sauce. Bring to a boil, then lower to a simmer, adding more stock as needed to keep the mixture soupy. Cook until the tortillas are well softened but not mushy. If desired, fry the eggs in a little butter in a small skillet. Serve the chilaquiles on two plates, topped with fried eggs, a dollop of sour cream, and a sprinkling of chopped cilantro.

Avocado "Sashimi" with Miso Dressing

▶ SERVES 2

1 ripe Hass avocado, halved, seeded, and flesh removed
1 lemon
1 teaspoon white or yellow miso
1 teaspoon grated fresh ginger
1 teaspoon light soy sauce
1 teaspoon sugar
1 teaspoon sesame oil
Wasabi paste for garnish
Pickled ginger for garnish

1. Place the avocado halves cut-side down on a board; score them at ⅛" intervals leaving the stem end connected to hold them together. Squeeze the lemon over the scored avocados to prevent browning. Fan the avocados onto two small plates.

2. In a small bowl, whisk together the miso, grated ginger, soy sauce, sugar, and sesame oil until the sugar is dissolved. Spoon some of the dressing over the avocados. Serve garnished with wasabi and pickled ginger.

Ratatouille

▶ SERVES 6

2 tablespoons olive oil
1 large onion, peeled and diced
2 medium zucchini, diced
2 medium yellow squash, diced
1 small eggplant, diced
1 medium bell pepper, seeded and diced
1 tablespoon flour
3 medium tomatoes, seeded and cut into 6 pieces
2 teaspoons dried herbes de Provence (or a combination of oregano, thyme, rosemary, marjoram, savory, and/or lavender)
1 teaspoon salt
Freshly ground black pepper
Chopped fresh basil leaves (optional)

1. Heat the olive oil in a heavy-bottomed Dutch oven until hot but not smoky. Add onion; cook until translucent, about 5 minutes. Combine the zucchini, yellow squash, eggplant, and bell pepper in a large paper or ziplock bag; dust with flour, fold or zip bag closed, and shake to coat. Add floured vegetables to the pot along with the tomatoes, herbes de Provence, salt, and pepper.

2. Reduce heat to a simmer, cover, and cook gently 1 hour until all vegetables are tender. Serve hot or at room temperature. Garnish with freshly chopped basil if desired.

Quick Tomato and Oregano Sauté

▶ SERVES 4

1 tablespoon olive oil

2 cloves garlic, peeled and finely minced

2 cups chopped tomatoes (any variety)

Scant ½ teaspoon salt

2 tablespoons chopped fresh oregano or ½ teaspoon dried

Freshly ground black pepper to taste

1. Heat olive oil in 10" skillet over medium heat. Sprinkle in chopped garlic and stir with a wooden spoon for only a moment until the garlic whitens and releases its aroma. Do not allow it to brown.

2. Add chopped tomato, salt, and if you are using dried oregano, add that now. Simmer 10 minutes until most water has evaporated, stirring occasionally.

3. Season with freshly ground black pepper, and if you are using fresh oregano, stir it in and simmer 1 minute more.

Basic Fresh Tomato Sauce

4 pounds tomatoes, preferably Roma plum tomatoes, but any variety will do

2 tablespoons olive oil

1 large onion, peeled and roughly chopped

5 cloves garlic, peeled and chopped (about 2 tablespoons)

1 teaspoon sugar

2 tablespoons tomato paste

Salt and freshly ground black pepper

1 cup washed fresh basil leaves, stems removed (optional)

1. Halve the tomatoes and squeeze out as many seeds as you can. Dice the tomatoes. Heat the olive oil in a large saucepan or Dutch oven (pan should be enamel, steel, or glass-lined—see Nonreactive Pots: Welcome to the Steel and Glass Generation sidebar in Chapter 7) over medium heat until hot enough to sizzle when a piece of onion is added. Add the onions; cook until soft and beginning to brown slightly, about 10 minutes. Stir in the garlic, sugar, and tomato paste; cook 2 minutes more, stirring constantly. Add the tomatoes; cook 10 minutes until mixture becomes brothy.

2. Uncover, lower heat to a slow simmer, and cook 30 minutes more until all tomatoes are fully softened; season with salt and pepper to taste. If you prefer chunky sauce, add the basil if desired. For smooth sauce, purée and strain, then add the basil leaves at the end.

Quick Tomato Sauce

▶ MAKES 1 QUART

2 tablespoons olive oil

1 medium onion, peeled and chopped

2 tablespoons chopped garlic (about 5 cloves)

1 teaspoon dried oregano (optional)

1 tablespoon tomato paste

1 teaspoon sugar

1 (28-ounce) can crushed tomatoes (use a domestic brand like Redpack, Progresso, Hunt's, or Muir Glen Organic—most imports in supermarkets are old and sour)

1 (14-ounce) can diced tomatoes in purée

Salt and freshly ground black pepper

Heat the oil in a medium saucepan 1 minute over medium heat. Add onions, garlic, and oregano if using; cook 5 minutes until onions are translucent. Stir in tomato paste and sugar; cook, stirring, 5 minutes more. Add crushed tomatoes, diced tomatoes, salt, and pepper. Simmer 10 minutes.

BEING CREATIVE WITH YOUR TOMATO SAUCE

There are many options available to you when preparing a tomato sauce. Try replacing the oregano with a bay leaf or some basil. Try a finely diced pepper or even cilantro in place of (or in addition to) the onion. Another idea is to look around the grocery store at what types of tomato sauces are there and take a crack at incorporating some of those varieties in your own sauce. Vodka and cream are also popular flavorings these days. Be sure to steam off any alcohol before adding vodka to tomato sauce.

Zucchini "Lasagna"

▶ SERVES 8

3 cups tomato sauce, divided

4 large zucchini, sliced very thin on a mandoline or slicing machine, about 1/8" thick

Kosher salt and freshly ground black pepper

1 pound ricotta cheese

1 pound provolone, fontina, mozzarella, or cheese of your choice, shredded

2 cups sautéed onions and mushrooms or 2 cups frozen mixed vegetables, thawed

ZUCCHINI LASAGNA TWIST

Try replacing about half the zucchini in this recipe with an equal portion of eggplant. Be sure to use thin, flat slices that are very lightly dusted on one side with salt.

1. Preheat oven to 350°F. Spread 1 cup sauce onto the bottom of a 9" × 13" baking dish. Arrange a layer of zucchini slices in the pan, overlapping the pieces by a third. Season with salt and pepper.

2. Dot the zucchini layer with half of the ricotta, distributing teaspoonfuls evenly around the casserole. Layer on 1/3 of the shredded cheese and half of the vegetables.

3. Arrange another layer of zucchini, season with salt and pepper, and repeat fillings using remaining ricotta, vegetables, and another third of the shredded cheese. Add a final layer of zucchini on top, season with salt and pepper, and spread on 2 more cups of tomato sauce.

4. Sprinkle top with remaining cheese; bake 1 hour until casserole is bubbly and cheese is lightly browned. Cool to room temperature and then refrigerate until cold. Cut into portions and reheat in the oven or microwave until hot.

Eggplant Rollatini

▶ SERVES 8

1 large eggplant, sliced lengthwise into even ⅛" slices (as thick as the cover of a hardcover book)

Flour for dredging

Egg wash of 6 large beaten eggs mixed with ½ cup water

4 cups bread crumbs

Oil for frying

1 pound ricotta cheese

8 ounces shredded mozzarella cheese

½ cup grated Parmesan (good quality, like Parmigiano-Reggiano or Grana Padano)

Salt and freshly ground black pepper

1½ pounds fresh spinach, washed and cooked, or 1 pound frozen spinach, thawed

4 cups tomato sauce

1. Bread and fry the eggplant: Dip a slice of eggplant in the flour to coat both sides; shake off excess flour, submerge in egg wash, shake off excess, and coat in bread crumbs, pressing to make sure they adhere well. Place on a holding tray and repeat with remaining slices. Heat oil to about 350°F (a piece of vegetable should sizzle visibly when dropped into the oil). Fry the breaded eggplant slices, dripping any excess oil off before stacking them between layers of paper towels.

2. Fill and roll: Preheat oven to 350°F. Combine all the cheeses in a medium mixing bowl and season lightly with salt and pepper. Place 1 teaspoon cooked spinach and a generous teaspoon of cheese mixture at the wide end of a fried eggplant slice. Roll away from yourself, jellyroll style, and place into a baking dish with the seam on the bottom. Repeat with remaining eggplant and fillings, lining the finished roulades close together in the baking dish. Bake until cheeses are visibly hot and the edges begin to brown lightly. Serve on a pool of tomato sauce garnished with basil leaves. Serve one piece per appetizer portion or two per main course.

Simple Salsa

MAKES 1 CUP

2 large tomatoes
1 small onion, peeled and finely diced
1 or 2 medium jalapeño peppers, seeded and finely chopped
½ teaspoon fresh-squeezed lime juice
Salt and freshly ground black pepper
½ teaspoon chipotle purée (optional)

Quarter the tomatoes. Cut out the inside viscera; reserve. Cut the remaining petals into a fine dice. Purée the insides in a blender or food processor until smooth. In a medium bowl, toss puréed tomatoes with the tomato dice, the diced onion, jalapeños, lime juice, salt, pepper, and chipotle if using. Keeps in the refrigerator for 2 days, but is best used the day it's made.

Green Bean and Pine Nut Sauté

SERVES 6

2 tablespoons extra-virgin olive oil
½ cup finely chopped shallots or red onion
¼ cup pine nuts
1 pound fresh green beans, blanched in salted water and shocked
1 cup diced tomatoes
Salt and freshly ground black pepper

Heat the oil in a large skillet over medium heat; add the shallots and pine nuts. Cook until the pine nuts begin to brown lightly, 3–4 minutes. Add the green beans, tomatoes, salt, and pepper. Cook only enough to warm through and soften the tomatoes slightly. Serve hot or at room temperature.

Eggplant Parmigiana

SERVES 8

Oil for frying
1 medium eggplant (about 1 pound), sliced thin
1 cup flour
3 large beaten eggs mixed with ½ cup water or milk
3 cups bread crumbs
4 cups tomato sauce
1 pound part-skim mozzarella cheese, shredded
Chopped fresh Italian parsley or whole fresh basil leaves

1. Heat the oil in a heavy skillet or fryer until a piece of vegetable sizzles when added. Dip a slice of eggplant in the flour and shake off excess, dip it in the egg mixture and shake off excess, and then press it into the bread crumbs. Repeat with remaining slices of eggplant. Fry the slices until golden, about 3 minutes each; drain on a rack or on paper towels.

2. Preheat oven to 350°F. Line the slices in a baking dish. Top each with 1 teaspoon tomato sauce and a small mound of shredded cheese. Bake until cheese is melted, brown, and bubbly, about 15 minutes. Serve with additional tomato sauce on the side garnished with chopped parsley or leaves of fresh basil.

Eggplant and Tomato Sauté

▶ SERVES 8

1 medium eggplant (about 1 pound), cut lengthwise into 8 wedges.
Kosher salt
3 tablespoons olive oil, divided
2 medium onions, peeled and sliced thickly (about ½")
¼ teaspoon crushed red pepper
1 tablespoon chopped garlic (about 3 cloves)
2 cups chopped plum tomatoes
¼ cup chopped fresh oregano or parsley

1. Sprinkle the eggplant wedges liberally with kosher salt; set aside 10–15 minutes until water visibly pools under the wedges (this extracts some bitter juices, making the eggplant especially mellow for this recipe). Dry the eggplant off with a towel. Heat 2 tablespoons olive oil in a large heavy-bottomed skillet until a piece of vegetable sizzles when added. Fry the eggplant wedges until they are lightly browned and bubbling with juice. Transfer to a cutting board and cut into large (2") pieces.

2. Put remaining olive oil in the skillet and heat 1 minute over medium heat. Add onions, crushed pepper, and garlic; cook, stirring occasionally, until onions are very soft, about 10 minutes. Add tomatoes and cook just until they begin to break down into a chunky sauce. Add the eggplant and chopped oregano or parsley. Bring to a simmer; remove from heat. Season to taste.

Steamed Asparagus with Hollandaise Sauce

▶ SERVES 6

3 large egg yolks

Juice of 1 lemon (about ¼ cup), divided

1 tablespoon plus a few drops of cold water, divided

8 ounces (2 sticks) melted butter

Pinch of cayenne pepper

¼ teaspoon salt

1 bunch asparagus, woody bottoms trimmed off

1. In a large, steel mixing bowl over a pot of simmering water or in a double boiler over very low heat, whisk together the yolks, half of the lemon juice, and 1 tablespoon cold water. Whisk vigorously until the yolks attain a lemon-yellow color and become thick (about the consistency of creamy salad dressing). Be careful not to let the eggs cook into lumps—keep whisking all the time and remove the bowl from the heat if it starts getting too hot. Once yolks are ready, set the bowl they are in onto a damp towel on a firm surface. Whisk in a few drops of cold water, then a few drops of the melted butter. Gradually whip in the melted butter in small increments, making sure that each addition is thoroughly incorporated before adding any more. Season with cayenne, salt, and remaining lemon juice.

2. Place asparagus in a microwave-safe dish and microwave 2–3 minutes until tender. Divide onto plates; spoon hollandaise over the middle of the stalks.

Roasted Asparagus with Mixed Summer Squash and Peppers

▶ SERVES 4

¼ cup olive oil

3 tablespoons balsamic vinegar

1 tablespoon minced garlic

1 pound asparagus, stem ends trimmed

1 pound mixed summer squash, thinly sliced

1 pound mini sweet peppers, stemmed, seeded, and sliced in half lengthwise

2–3 hot peppers, chopped

Seasoning salt to taste

1. Preheat oven to 400°F.

2. In a small bowl, mix the olive oil, balsamic vinegar, and garlic together and set aside.

3. Place the vegetables into a large roasting pan, mixing them together so the flavors will mingle. Pour the olive oil mixture over top, lifting and gently mixing the vegetables so they are all coated with oil. Sprinkle the vegetables with seasoning salt.

4. Roast the vegetables uncovered about 45 minutes or until they begin to darken; stir occasionally. Serve hot.

Asparagus-Shallot Sauté

▶ SERVES 6

1 bunch asparagus

Kosher salt

1 tablespoon olive oil or butter

½ cup finely chopped shallots (about 4 shallots)

Pinch of roughly freshly ground black pepper

Lemon wedges

1. Bring a large pot of water to a rolling boil and cook the asparagus until fully cooked but tender, about 2–4 minutes. Shock asparagus in a bowl of salted ice water, transfer to a cutting board and cut on a diagonal angle into 2" pieces.

2. Heat the olive oil in a large skillet over medium heat; add the shallots and black pepper. Cook until translucent, about 3 minutes; add the asparagus and cook until heated through. Season to taste. Serve with lemon wedges on the side.

HOW TO MAKE LEMON WEDGES

Waiters and bartenders drive chefs nuts when they try to get artistic with citrus. Chopping off the ends of the lemons, cutting wedges super thin, cutting the limes into slices instead of wedges—these unnecessary steps all lead to inconvenient and messy squeezes. Select lemons and limes that are as elongated as possible for wedges. Then, just halve, quarter, and eighth the fruit lengthwise. Flick out only the seeds you see on the surface of the wedges using the tip of a small knife. Don't bother mining for deep seeds—it'll only yield sloppy wedges.

Roasted Vegetables

▶ SERVES 8

1 small eggplant (about 1 pound), cubed

1 small butternut squash (about 1½ pounds), peeled and cubed

1 pound red potatoes, cubed

3 large "horse" carrots or approximately 1 pound cello carrots, cut into 1"
pieces

12 cloves garlic, peeled

2 large white onions, peeled and cut into 1" cubes

1 medium zucchini and 1 yellow squash, cubed

10 ounces mushrooms

3 tablespoons olive oil

1 teaspoon kosher salt

½ teaspoon freshly ground black pepper

½ cup mixed chopped fresh herbs (rosemary, thyme, oregano, parsley,
chives) or less than ¼ cup dried mixed herbs

¼ cup good-quality balsamic vinegar

1. Preheat oven to 350°F. In a large bowl, combine eggplant, butternut
squash, potatoes, carrots, garlic, onions, zucchini, yellow squash,
mushrooms, olive oil, salt, pepper, and mixed herbs; toss to coat.

2. Spread into a single layer onto one or two roasting pans, jellyroll pans,
or baking dishes. Cook 1–1½ hours until vegetables are very tender
and browned lightly. Sprinkle with balsamic vinegar and set out to
cool.

Chinese Wrinkled String Beans

▶ SERVES 4

Oil for deep-frying
1 pound fresh green beans, stem ends snipped off
2 tablespoons peanut oil
½ cup chopped scallions
1 (1") piece fresh ginger, peeled and finely chopped
1 tablespoon chopped garlic
1 teaspoon sugar
1 teaspoon white vinegar
Salt
Sesame oil

1. Heat 2" of oil in a wok or deep skillet to 350°F (a piece of vegetable should sizzle vigorously, but the oil should not smoke). Carefully fry the green beans in four small batches. They will shrivel as they cook—they take about 5 minutes per batch. Leave time in between batches to let the oil come back up to temperature.

2. In a separate large skillet, heat the peanut oil. Add the scallions, ginger, garlic, sugar, and vinegar. Cook 1 minute until the garlic turns white. Add the green beans; toss to coat. Season with salt and sesame oil.

Stir-Fried Snow Peas with Cilantro

▶ SERVES 4

2 tablespoons peanut or other light oil

1 cup thinly sliced scallions

1 cup snow peas

½ cup Vegetable Stock (see recipe in Chapter 5)

2 teaspoons cornstarch

2 tablespoons cold water

½ cup finely chopped fresh cilantro

Dash of soy sauce

Pinch of sugar

1. Heat oil in a large skillet until very hot, almost smoking. Add scallions and snow peas; toss or stir quickly to coat them with oil. Add stock, cover the skillet, and cook 2 minutes. Meanwhile, in a small bowl, mix the cornstarch with 2 tablespoons cold water and the cilantro.

2. Stir the cornstarch mixture quickly into the peas, stirring constantly until the sauce thickens; season with soy sauce and sugar. Serve immediately. The entire cooking time for the peas should not exceed 5 minutes.

Peck of Peppers Tart

▶ SERVES 6

2 tablespoons olive oil
1 tablespoon minced garlic
2 cups coarsely chopped peppers of your choice
4 large eggs, beaten
1 cup milk
1 cup shredded Swiss cheese
2 teaspoons smoked paprika
Salt and freshly ground black pepper to taste
1 (9") deep-dish pie crust

1. Preheat oven to 350°F.
2. Heat the oil in a large skillet over medium heat and sauté the garlic 30 seconds. Add the peppers and sauté 2–3 minutes.
3. In a medium bowl, mix the eggs, milk, cheese, paprika, salt, and pepper together until well combined. Stir in the peppers and pour the mixture into the pie crust.
4. Bake the tart 30 minutes or until the center is firm and the top browns. Serve hot.

Turkish-Style Stuffed Pepper

▶ SERVES 1

1 large red bell pepper
Olive oil
½ cup cooked brown rice
¼ cup soy "meat" crumbles
2 tablespoons raisins
2 tablespoons chopped dried apricots
2 tablespoons chopped fresh mint
2 tablespoons chopped fresh parsley
2 tablespoons plain yogurt

1. Preheat oven to 400°F.
2. Cut the top off the pepper and clean out the seeds and membranes. Rub the pepper inside and out with the olive oil.
3. In a medium bowl, combine the rice with the soy "meat," raisins, apricots, mint, parsley, and yogurt. Carefully spoon the mixture into the hollow pepper. Prop the pepper upright in a baking dish.
4. Bake the pepper 30 minutes or until the pepper is tender. Serve.

Zucchini Ragout

▶ SERVES 6

5 ounces fresh spinach

3 medium zucchini, diced

½ cup diced red onion

2 stalks celery, diced

2 medium carrots, peeled and diced

1 medium parsnip, peeled and diced

3 tablespoons tomato paste

¼ cup water

1 teaspoon freshly ground black pepper

¼ teaspoon kosher salt

1 tablespoon minced fresh basil

1 tablespoon minced fresh Italian parsley

1 tablespoon minced fresh oregano

SAVING ON HERBS

The cost of herbs can add up quickly, but you can save a little money by shopping at an international farmers' market or buying a blend of spices (an Italian blend would work well in this recipe) instead of buying each individually.

Place all ingredients into a 4-quart slow cooker. Stir. Cook on low 4 hours. Stir before serving.

PASTA, GRAIN, AND RICE DISHES

Sun-Dried Tomato Risotto with Spinach and Pine Nuts

▶ SERVES 4

1 medium yellow onion, peeled and diced

4 cloves garlic, peeled and minced

2 tablespoons olive oil

1½ cups Arborio rice

5–6 cups vegetable broth

⅔ cup rehydrated sliced sun-dried tomatoes

½ cup fresh spinach

1 tablespoon chopped fresh basil (optional)

2 tablespoons vegan margarine (optional)

2 tablespoons nutritional yeast

Salt and freshly ground black pepper to taste

¼ cup pine nuts

SUN-DRIED TOMATOES

If you're using dehydrated tomatoes, rehydrate them first by covering in water at least 10 minutes, and add the soaking water to the broth. If you're using tomatoes packed in oil, add 2 tablespoons of the oil to risotto at the end of cooking instead of the vegan margarine.

1. In a large skillet, heat onion and garlic in olive oil until just soft, about 2–3 minutes. Add rice and toast 1 minute, stirring constantly.

2. Add ¾ cup vegetable broth and stir to combine. When most of the liquid has been absorbed, add another ½ cup, stirring constantly. Continue adding liquid ½ cup at a time until rice is cooked, about 20 minutes.

3. Add another ½ cup broth, tomatoes, and spinach and reduce heat to low. Stir to combine well. Heat 3–4 minutes until tomatoes are soft and spinach is wilted.

4. Stir in basil, margarine, and nutritional yeast. Taste, then season lightly with a bit of salt and pepper.

5. Allow to cool slightly, then top with pine nuts. Risotto will thicken a bit as it cools.

Spanish Artichoke and Zucchini Paella

▶ SERVES 4

3 cloves garlic, peeled and minced

1 medium yellow onion, peeled and diced

2 tablespoons olive oil

1 cup white rice

1 (15-ounce) can diced or crushed tomatoes

1 medium green bell pepper, seeded and chopped

1 medium red or yellow bell pepper, seeded and chopped

½ cup chopped artichoke hearts

2 zucchini, sliced

2 cups vegetable broth

1 tablespoon paprika

½ teaspoon ground turmeric

¾ teaspoon dried parsley

½ teaspoon salt

1. In a paella pan or the largest skillet you can find, heat garlic and onions in olive oil 3–4 minutes until onions are almost soft. Add rice and stir well to coat; heat another minute while stirring to prevent burning.

2. Add tomatoes, bell peppers, artichokes, and zucchini; stir to combine. Add vegetable broth and remaining ingredients, cover, and simmer 15–20 minutes or until rice is done.

Vegan Stroganoff

▶ SERVES 4

1 tablespoon olive oil

2 (14-ounce) packages extra-firm tofu, crumbled

1 medium yellow onion, peeled and minced

1 cup sliced mushrooms

1 teaspoon garlic powder

2 tablespoons low-sodium soy sauce

1 (12-ounce) container nonfat cottage cheese

2 tablespoons plain low-fat Greek-style yogurt or soy yogurt

16 ounces 100% whole-wheat noodles, cooked

2 teaspoons freshly ground black pepper

THE CLEAN ANSWER TO HEAVY CREAM

Packed with fat and calories, heavily processed, and possibly containing hormones, antibiotics, and steroids, heavy dairy cream is a clean-eating nightmare! In recipes that include this classic creamy recipe staple, the clean-eating vegetarian knows that plain Greek-style yogurt, or vegan yogurt thickened with ground flaxseed, can serve as a perfect protein-packed substitute to the unhealthy alternative.

1. Prepare a large skillet with olive oil over medium heat.

2. Sauté tofu crumbles and onion in the olive oil 7 minutes or until cooked through.

3. Add the mushrooms, garlic powder, and soy sauce and combine well.

4. Stir in the cottage cheese and Greek yogurt until the ingredients become a thick sauce. Remove from the heat.

5. In a large bowl, combine the cooked noodles, tofu mixture, and pepper and blend well. Serve immediately.

Red Pepper Rice with Mushrooms and Sweet Peas

▶ SERVES 2

Olive oil spray

2 medium red bell peppers, seeded and chopped

2 cups sliced baby portobello mushrooms

½ cup balsamic vinegar, divided

2 teaspoons maple syrup

2 cups cooked brown rice

2 cups sweet peas

1. Heat a large skillet over medium heat and spray with olive oil spray. Add the red peppers, mushrooms, ¼ cup balsamic vinegar, and maple syrup. Sauté until red peppers are cooked and mushrooms are softened.

2. Add cooked rice and remaining ¼ cup of balsamic and sauté together until cooked through and combined, about 4–5 minutes.

3. Add peas and sauté until cooked thoroughly, about 2 minutes, and remove from heat.

WHAT MAKES A CARBOHYDRATE "GOOD" OR "BAD"?

Refined carbs are those like white breads, cakes, pastries, and countless other varieties of processed goods that include "refined," or treated, ingredients. Whole grains are carbohydrates that, while processed, contain grains that are minimally processed in order to retain the whole natural wheat-berry, which is the powerhouse of wheat's nutrition. Complex carbohydrates are those most commonly found in nature, like fruits and vegetables. Good carbs are those that have been processed the least . . . and taste great in their natural state; bad carbs are those that have been messed with the most . . . and wouldn't really taste that great otherwise.

Balsamic Green Beans with Quinoa

▶ SERVES 2

2 cups trimmed and halved green beans

1 cup balsamic vinegar, divided

2 teaspoons maple syrup

2 cups cooked quinoa

1 teaspoon all-natural sea salt

1 teaspoon freshly ground black pepper

1. In a large sauté pan over medium heat, combine the green beans, ½ cup balsamic, and maple syrup and cook until green beans are tender. Add 1 tablespoon of water as needed to assist with cooking and prevent balsamic from evaporating.

2. Add the quinoa and remaining balsamic to the sauté pan and sauté until thoroughly combined.

3. Remove from heat and add salt and pepper.

GREEN BEANS CONTAIN CAROTENOIDS, TOO!

Most people think of carrots and tomatoes as the top providers of carotenoids like lutein and beta carotene, but a fun fact about green beans is that they, too, boast bountiful amounts of these disease-fighting phytochemicals. Green beans contain the most well-known carotenoids like lutein and beta carotene that work wonders on protecting the health of the skin and eyes while also providing amazing antioxidants, vitamins, and minerals that serve to protect and promote the whole body's systems and every unit that comprises them . . . down to the smallest of cells.

Asian Tofu Sauté with Rice Noodles

▶ SERVES 2

1 (14-ounce) package extra-firm tofu, cubed

2 tablespoons sesame oil, divided

1 cup chopped green onions

1 clove garlic, peeled and minced

2 cups cooked rice noodles

2 tablespoons rice wine vinegar

½ cup toasted sesame seeds

1 teaspoon all-natural sea salt

LITTLE POWERHOUSE PREVENTERS OF BAD CHOLESTEROL

Sesame seeds not only taste great, pair well with almost every food, and have such low fat, calories, sodium, sugar, etc., that it would be ridiculous not to keep them on hand, but they also help promote healthy cholesterol levels. By toting healthy phytosterols, plant compounds that are similar to cholesterol, sesame seeds can help improve healthy cholesterol (HDL) in the blood and reduce bad cholesterol (LDL) at the same time.

1. In a large sauté pan over medium heat, sauté the tofu and 1 tablespoon of sesame oil until tofu is cooked through and slightly crunchy, about 6–8 minutes.

2. Add the green onions, garlic, and remaining tablespoon of sesame oil and sauté 3–4 minutes more.

3. Add the cooked rice noodles and rice wine vinegar and toss to combine thoroughly and heat noodles.

4. Remove from heat, plate, and sprinkle with toasted sesame seeds and salt.

Sweet Rice and Sweeter Peppers

▶ SERVES 2

1 medium red pepper, seeded and cut
    into ¼" squares

1 medium yellow pepper, seeded and cut
    into ¼" squares

2 medium sweet peppers, seeded and
    cut into ¼" squares

1 cup coconut milk, divided

2 teaspoons maple syrup, divided

2 cups cooked brown rice

1 teaspoon all-natural sea salt

1. In a large skillet over medium heat,
   cook the pepper chunks in ¼ cup of
   the coconut milk and 1 teaspoon of
   the maple syrup until softened but
   still crisp, about 4–6 minutes.

2. Add the cooked rice, remaining
   coconut milk, and remaining
   teaspoon of maple syrup. Stir together
   until well-blended and heated
   through.

3. Remove from heat and add salt.

MAPLE SYRUP FOR A QUICK, LOW DOSE OF SWEETNESS

While maple syrup has a very unique taste that packs intense sweetness, its flavor is not such an overpowering essence that it has to be limited to only pancakes and oatmeal. Because of its concentrated sweetness, maple syrup is a great ingredient to use in everyday dishes because a little goes a long way and that teaspoon or two has fewer calories and far more vitamins and minerals than its sweet alternatives.

Slow-Cooker Paella

▶ SERVES 6

1 tablespoon olive oil

½ medium onion, peeled and diced

1 cup diced tomato

½ teaspoon saffron or ground turmeric

1 teaspoon salt

2 tablespoons chopped fresh parsley

1 cup long-grain white rice

1 cup frozen peas

2 cups water

1 (12-ounce) package vegan chorizo, crumbled

1. Heat the olive oil in a sauté pan over medium heat. Add the onion and sauté 3 minutes.

2. Add the tomato, saffron, salt, and parsley and stir.

3. Pour the sautéed mixture into a 4-quart slow cooker. Add the white rice, then frozen peas and water.

4. Cover and cook on low heat 4 hours.

5. Pour the crumbled chorizo on top of the rice. Cover and cook an additional 30 minutes. Stir before serving.

Wild Mushroom Risotto

SERVES 2

1 tablespoon olive oil

1 medium yellow onion, peeled and minced

2 tablespoons minced garlic

1⅓ cups long-grain brown rice

3¾ cups water

6 cups quartered baby portobello mushrooms

1 teaspoon all-natural sea salt

1 teaspoon freshly ground black pepper

2 teaspoons Italian seasoning

RISOTTO'S BAD RAP

Many people don't make their own risotto because it's rumored to be so difficult: too wet, too dry, too sticky, or not sticky enough. But just stir constantly, use fresh ingredients, and watch closely for all the water to be absorbed, and you'll create a delicious risotto every time.

1. Drizzle the olive oil in a saucepan over medium heat and sauté the minced onion and garlic until softened, about 5 minutes.

2. Add the uncooked rice to the saucepan and turn to coat in the oil, garlic, and onions. Stir over heat 2 minutes.

3. Add the water, mushrooms, and seasonings to the saucepan and stir to combine.

4. Bring to a boil, reduce heat to low, and simmer uncovered 20 minutes, stirring frequently.

5. Risotto is done when the rice has absorbed all of the liquid and is sticky but cooked through.

Slow-Cooker Red Beans and Rice

▶ SERVES 4

3 cups water

3½ cups Vegetable Stock (see recipe in Chapter 5)

2 tablespoons butter or vegan margarine

1 (15-ounce) can kidney beans, drained

2 cups uncooked white rice

1 medium onion, peeled and chopped

1 medium green bell pepper, seeded and chopped

1 cup chopped celery

1 teaspoon dried thyme

1 teaspoon paprika

1 teaspoon Cajun seasoning

½ teaspoon crushed red pepper

1 teaspoon salt

¼ teaspoon freshly ground black pepper

RECIPE VARIATIONS FOR COMPLETELY DIFFERENT TASTE SENSATIONS

For a heartier vegetarian meal, you can always add sliced vegetarian sausage or vegetarian beef crumbles during the last hour of cooking.

1. Combine all ingredients in a 4-quart slow cooker.

2. Cover and cook on low heat 6 hours.

3. If the rice is tender, remove from heat. If the rice is not cooked through and tender, cook an additional hour.

Vegetarian Lasagna

▶ SERVES 12

2 (8-ounce) packages 100% whole-wheat
    lasagna noodles

1 tablespoon olive oil

1 small zucchini, sliced thinly

1 medium green pepper, seeded and
    diced

3 teaspoons minced garlic

1 medium yellow onion, peeled and
    minced

1 pound sliced portobello mushrooms

6 cups tomato sauce

4 teaspoons Italian seasoning, divided

2 large eggs or ½ cup egg substitute

1 cup cottage cheese

1 cup plain low-fat Greek-style yogurt or
    soy yogurt

12 thin slices fresh buffalo mozzarella or
    vegan mozzarella

DITCH THE PROCESSED CHEESE

The clean lifestyle makes a major point of still eating things you love, but trying to use fresh ingredients and healthier alternatives whenever possible. Cheese is one thing that's common in the standard American diet that really shouldn't be. Heavily processed, fat-packed, calorie-laden, dairy cheeses like deli slices and prepackaged singles are terribly unnatural. Fresh buffalo mozzarella and crumbled goat cheese are two natural alternatives that are very versatile, minimally processed, and taste great. These are two healthy options you can live with.

1. Preheat oven to 350°F and prepare a 9" × 13" baking dish with olive oil spray.

2. Bring a large pot with water over medium-high heat to boil. Cook noodles until al dente, remove, rinse, and cool.

3. Prepare the rinsed noodle pot with 1 tablespoon olive oil and add the zucchini, pepper, minced garlic, and onion. Sauté 2–3 minutes, then add the mushrooms, sauce, and half of the Italian seasoning. Reduce heat to medium and simmer 15 minutes.

4. Combine the eggs, cottage cheese, and yogurt in a mixing bowl.

5. Pour 1 cup of the sauce in the bottom of the dish to coat. Layer (for two layers) half of the noodles, followed by half of the sauce, dollops of the yogurt mix spread, and half of the mozzarella cheese.

6. Layer in the same order for a second time and sprinkle the mozzarella topping with remaining Italian seasoning.

7. Bake 30–45 minutes or until bubbly and cooked through.

Tofu Spaghetti

SERVES 4

1 tablespoon olive oil

1 (14-ounce) package extra-firm tofu, crumbled

2 cups tomato sauce

4 cups cooked 100% whole-wheat spaghetti

2 teaspoons all-natural sea salt

4 slices fresh buffalo mozzarella or vegan mozzarella

¼ cup chopped fresh basil

WHO NEEDS MEAT WHEN YOU'VE GOT TOFU?

The blank taste of tofu is a wonderful thing when it comes to substitutions for meat in traditionally meaty dishes. Versatile because of its ability to take on flavors of strong ingredients, tofu's appeal doesn't end there. Able to be used as chunks that rival meat crumbles, the soy product is hearty enough to be used as a healthier alternative to ground beef in all of your favorite dishes.

1. In a large skillet over medium heat, combine the olive oil and crumbled tofu and sauté until slightly browned.

2. Add the tomato sauce to the sautéed tofu and bring to a simmer.

3. Remove the tofu and sauce from the heat and move to a large serving bowl and thoroughly combine with the pasta and salt.

4. Plate and garnish with the mozzarella slices and chopped basil.

White Lasagna with Spinach and Mushrooms

▶ SERVES 12

5 cups milk

1 large onion, peeled and roughly chopped

2 bay leaves

4 whole cloves

Pinch of ground nutmeg

6 ounces (1½ sticks) unsalted butter

¾ cup flour

Salt and white pepper

1 (1-pound) package no-boil lasagna noodles (or parboiled regular lasagna)

1 pound ricotta

1 cup grated Parmigiano-Reggiano or other top-quality Parmesan cheese

1½ pounds shredded provolone, Monterey jack, or mozzarella cheese

1 pound mixed mushrooms (white, shiitake, cremini, portobello, etc.), sliced, seasoned, and sautéed

1½ pounds fresh spinach (or 1 pound frozen chopped spinach, thawed), cooked

1. Prepare the white sauce: Combine the milk, onion, bay leaves, cloves, and nutmeg in a small saucepan; simmer slowly 10 minutes.

2. In a medium saucepan, melt the butter, stir in the flour, and cook on medium heat until it smells slightly nutty, bubbles slightly, but has not darkened in color at all, about 3 minutes.

3. Strain the milk; gradually whisk the strained milk into the bubbling flour mixture, whisking out any lumps that may form.

4. Simmer 10 minutes; season with salt and white pepper.

5. Assemble the lasagna: Preheat oven to 350°F. Spread 2 cups of white sauce on the bottom of a 9" × 13" baking dish. Arrange a layer of lasagna noodles onto the sauce; dot it with spoonfuls of ricotta (half of total) and a sprinkling of each of the other cheeses (⅓ of each). Form another noodle layer on top of the cheese. Distribute all of the cooked mushrooms and spinach in a single layer, season with salt and pepper, sprinkle with another third of the grated and shredded cheeses, and dot with the remaining ricotta. Top with a final layer of noodle, smooth on another 2 cups of white sauce, and sprinkle with remaining cheeses.

6. Bake until bubbly and browned on top, about 25 minutes. Rest at room temperature 10 minutes before cutting into twelve servings. Serve the remaining white sauce on the side.

Tomato-Basil Rigatoni

▶ SERVES 2

2 cups cooked 100% whole-wheat rigatoni pasta

2 cups tomato sauce

1 teaspoon garlic powder

¼ cup chopped fresh basil

2 tablespoons Italian seasoning

½ cup crumbled fresh buffalo mozzarella or vegan mozzarella

1. In a large mixing bowl, combine the hot cooked pasta with the tomato sauce, garlic powder, chopped basil, and Italian seasoning.

2. Plate pasta and sprinkle the mozzarella crumbles over top.

SPICE IT UP!

If you're looking to jazz up a dish you fear might be on the bland side, don't reach for that salt! Rather than using sodium (which is already consumed in high amounts in many diets), fresh and dried herbs can lend a lot of taste without any of the sodium. Basil, rosemary, oregano, tarragon, cumin, cilantro, turmeric, and many more can be the pleasant pairing you're looking for!

Pumpkin-Spinach Lasagna

▶ SERVES 8

1 pound lasagna

1 tablespoon salt

1 small (2–3 pounds) pumpkin

¼ teaspoon crushed red pepper

¼ teaspoon ground nutmeg

2 tablespoons olive oil

3 cloves garlic, peeled and chopped

1 large bunch spinach (or cello bag), washed thoroughly

Salt and freshly ground black pepper to taste

2 pounds ricotta

1 large egg

4 ounces grated Parmesan

4 ounces grated mozzarella or provolone cheese

2 cups tomato sauce

1. Cook lasagna according to directions on box (it's best to undercook a little). Rinse and drain. Toss with a drop of olive oil. Set aside. Refill pasta pot with 3 quarts water, add 1 tablespoon salt, and bring to boil.

2. Preheat oven to 400°F. Peel pumpkin (cut off the top and bottom and shave the outside with a knife, always shaving downward toward the cutting board; you may find a potato peeler easier), discard seeds, and cube into bite-sized pieces. Boil pumpkin pieces 15 minutes until tender in salted water. Drain and toss with crushed pepper and nutmeg.

3. In a 10" skillet, sauté half of the garlic in 1 tablespoon olive oil; add half of the spinach when garlic starts to brown. Allow spinach to wilt, then turn out onto a plate and repeat with remaining oil, spinach, and garlic. Season with salt and pepper. Mix the ricotta, egg, and Parmesan together. Set aside.

4. Assemble the lasagna in layers in a 9" × 13" baking dish, starting with noodles, then cheese mixture, then spinach and pumpkin. Make two more layers, making sure to save unbroken lasagna for the top layer. Sprinkle grated mozzarella or provolone on top.

5. Bake 30 minutes until brown and bubbling on top. Let rest 15 minutes before serving with tomato sauce on the side.

Baked Veggie Pasta

SERVES 5

2 cups chopped spinach
3 medium roasted red peppers, sliced
2 cups sliced portobello mushrooms
2 cups quartered artichoke hearts
½ medium red onion, peeled and sliced
1 zucchini, sliced into ¼" rounds
2 cups sliced black olives
2 cups crumbled goat cheese or vegan soft cheese
4 cups cooked 100% whole-wheat penne pasta

1. Prepare a 9" × 13" baking dish with olive oil spray and preheat oven to 350°F.

2. In a mixing bowl, combine the spinach, red peppers, mushrooms, artichoke hearts, onion, zucchini, olives, and cheese. Fold in the pasta and combine well.

3. Pour the vegetable pasta mixture into the prepared baking dish and bake 30–45 minutes.

Pasta Primavera

4 tablespoons olive oil, divided
1 small zucchini, sliced
1 small yellow squash, sliced
1 medium yellow onion, peeled and sliced
1 large carrot, peeled and sliced
4 tablespoons water (as needed)
1 cup sliced baby portobello mushrooms
½ medium red pepper, seeded and chopped
1 cup broccoli florets
4 cups cooked 100% whole-wheat rigatoni pasta
2 teaspoons garlic powder
2 teaspoons freshly ground black pepper
2 teaspoons all-natural sea salt
1 teaspoon onion powder

1. Prepare a skillet with 1 tablespoon of olive oil over medium heat and sauté the zucchini, squash, onion, and carrots about 7 minutes, adding water when needed to prevent sticking and promote steaming.

2. Add mushrooms, red pepper, and broccoli and continue to sauté another 7 minutes or until all vegetables are slightly softened.

3. Pour the prepared pasta into a mixing bowl and add vegetables and seasonings. Drizzle remaining 2–3 tablespoons of olive oil (for desired taste) over the pasta and toss to coat.

Summer Squash Casserole

SERVES 8

1 large zucchini, cut into bite-sized pieces
1 large yellow squash, peeled and cut into bite-sized pieces
1 butternut squash, peeled and cut into bite-sized pieces
2 tablespoons olive oil
2 tablespoons Italian seasoning
1 tablespoon paprika
2 teaspoons all-natural sea salt
2 cups cooked brown rice
½ cup crumbled goat cheese or vegan soft cheese

1. Preheat oven to 400°F and prepare a 9" × 13" baking dish with olive oil spray.
2. In a large mixing bowl, combine the squash, olive oil, and seasonings and mix well.
3. Fold in the rice and goat cheese and bake 35–45 minutes or until cooked through and bubbly.

VERSATILE DELICIOUSNESS

If you're looking for a wonderful fresh vegetable that can be made creamy, crunchy, sweet, or salty, look no further than summer squash. Blended with fresh ingredients, natural nectars, or light and savory seasonings, you can create the most amazing-tasting dishes. Whether you'd like a sautéed dish, a hearty casserole, or a creamy soup, summer squash is an easy, inexpensive ingredient that makes for a delicious and nutritious meal any day or night of the week.

Linguine with Fire-Roasted Tomatoes, Basil, and Mozzarella

▶ SERVES 2

2 cups fire-roasted tomatoes

1½ tablespoons extra-virgin olive oil, divided

½ cup chopped fresh basil

4 ounces buffalo mozzarella or vegan mozzarella, cubed in ¼" cubes

2 cups cooked 100% whole-wheat linguine

1 teaspoon garlic powder

1 teaspoon all-natural sea salt

1 teaspoon freshly ground black pepper

1. In a large bowl, combine the fire-roasted tomatoes, 1 tablespoon olive oil, basil, and mozzarella. Toss well to combine and thoroughly coat with the olive oil.

2. Add the cooked linguine to the tomatoes, basil, and mozzarella and fold gently to combine.

3. Add the garlic, salt, and pepper, and remaining olive oil as needed to prevent spices from clumping. Mix well to distribute spices evenly throughout. Serve or refrigerate to allow flavors to marry.

EAT LIKE A CAVEMAN

In the earliest times, mankind depended on the land for nourishment. When they weren't hunting for meat, diets consisted of vegetation. Researchers believe that these earliest civilizations knew to seek out the brightest of fruits and vegetables for the majority of their diets, not just because of taste but because of the long-lasting energy that resulted. Quick, easy, and beneficial, bright foods were the crux of a healthy diet even long ago.

Cheesy Spinach Shells

▶ SERVES 2

2 cups spinach

2 cups cottage cheese or vegan cottage cheese

¼ cup ground flaxseed

4 ounces crumbled goat cheese or vegan soft cheese

1 garlic clove, chopped

1 teaspoon garlic powder

1 teaspoon all-natural sea salt

1 teaspoon freshly ground black pepper

6 cooked 100% whole-wheat pasta shells

SNEAK SPINACH IN ANY DISH

Green smoothies aren't the only place spinach can hide. Chopped or left in whole leaves, spinach can be scattered throughout almost any dish for a boost of essential vitamins and minerals without an overpowering taste that throws off a dish's design. Beautifully colored and one of the most nutritious leafy vegetables, spinach is the perfect ingredient to top your list but hide from taste buds.

1. Preheat oven to 350°F and prepare a 9" × 9" dish with olive oil spray.

2. In a large bowl, mix the spinach, cottage cheese, ground flaxseed, goat cheese, and chopped garlic until thoroughly combined. Add garlic powder, sea salt, and pepper.

3. Place the shells into the prepared dish seam-side up and stuff each shell full of the spinach and cottage cheese mixture.

4. Cover the dish and bake 30–35 minutes. Remove cover and continue to bake 10–15 minutes or until shells are firm and stuffing is bubbly.

Great Greens Pasta Pot

▶ SERVES 2

2 cups broccoli florets
2 cups green beans
2 cups sweet peas
½ cup water
¼ cup lemon juice
2 cups cooked 100% whole-wheat penne pasta
¼ cup goat cheese or vegan soft cheese
1 teaspoon all-natural sea salt
1 teaspoon freshly ground black pepper

1. In a large skillet over medium heat, combine the broccoli, green beans, and sweet peas with enough water to completely cover the bottom of the skillet. Sauté together until water evaporates and broccoli and green beans are slightly softened but still crisp, about 5–6 minutes. Douse the vegetables with the lemon juice and sauté 1 minute more.

2. Add the cooked pasta to the skillet and sauté with the vegetables until heated through. Add the goat cheese and cook 1–2 minutes or until the goat cheese has softened.

3. Remove from heat, stir well to combine, and season with salt and pepper.

Cheesy Mushroom and Sweet Pea Pasta

▶ SERVES 2

1 tablespoon extra-virgin olive oil

2 cups chopped baby portobello mushrooms

1 teaspoon all-natural sea salt, divided

1 teaspoon freshly ground black pepper, divided

2 cups petite sweet peas

¼ cup freshly squeezed lemon juice

1 cup crumbled goat cheese

2 cups cooked 100% whole-wheat rotini pasta

1 cup nonfat Greek-style yogurt or soy yogurt

1 teaspoon garlic powder

PASTA SUGGESTIONS

If you prefer one type of pasta over another, you can always make substitutions to alter a recipe to better suit your tastes. Replacing a thin spaghetti with a thicker linguine, rotini for small shells, or any other variations are up to the creative consumer. The only things to bear in mind are the sauce and ingredients that accompany your pasta, and how well they will blend with the type of pasta of your choosing.

1. Prepare a large skillet over medium heat with the tablespoon of olive oil. Sauté the mushrooms with ½ teaspoon each of the sea salt and black pepper. Cook 3–5 minutes or until cooked through and reduced. Add the sweet peas, lemon juice, and goat cheese to the skillet and heat through 1 minute or until a smooth sauce develops. Add the cooked rotini, warm the pasta for 1 minute, and remove from heat.

2. Stir in the yogurt to combine thoroughly and season with remaining salt and pepper and garlic powder.

Fusilli (Spirals) with Grilled Eggplant, Garlic, and Spicy Tomato Sauce

▶ SERVES 4

1 small eggplant (about half a pound), cut lengthwise into 8 wedges
3 tablespoons olive oil, divided
Kosher salt and freshly ground black pepper
3 cloves garlic, finely chopped (about 1 tablespoon)
¼ teaspoon crushed red pepper
½ cup roughly chopped fresh Italian parsley
4 cups tomato sauce
½ box (½ pound) fusilli or other pasta shape, cooked al dente
1 tablespoon butter (optional)
¼ cup grated vegan Parmesan cheese (optional)

1. Heat grill, grill pan, or broiler. Toss the eggplant wedges with 1 tablespoon olive oil; season liberally with salt and pepper. Grill or broil them on the largest cut side 4 minutes until black marks show. Using tongs or a fork, turn to another side and cook 3 minutes more until they are bubbling with juices. Transfer to a cutting board to cool; cut into 1" pieces.

2. In a small bowl, mix remaining olive oil with garlic and red pepper. Heat a large skillet over medium-high heat. Add the garlic mixture; allow to sizzle just 15 seconds, stirring with a wooden spoon. Add the parsley and cook 30 seconds; add the eggplant and tomato sauce. Bring to a simmer, add the cooked pasta, and cook until heated through; remove from heat. Finish by adding butter and cheese (if using), adjust seasoning with salt and pepper, and toss well to combine. Serve in bowls and sprinkle with additional chopped parsley. Pass additional cheese on the side if desired.

Gemelli with Asparagus Tips, Lemon, and Butter

▶ SERVES 4

2 bunches medium asparagus, cut on bias into 1½" pieces
½ pound gemelli pasta
4 tablespoons unsalted butter, divided
Juice and zest of 2 lemons
½ cup Vegetable Stock (see recipe in Chapter 5) or water
Salt and freshly ground black pepper to taste
Grated Parmesan

1. Parboil the asparagus pieces in three batches in a large pot with 6 quarts rapidly boiling salted water, about 2–4 minutes each batch; plunge asparagus pieces immediately into a large bowl of salted ice water as they are removed from cooking water, then drain. Boil gemelli in the asparagus cooking water until al dente (soft but still slightly chewy in the center), about 10–12 minutes. Drain and rinse.

2. Melt 1 tablespoon butter in a skillet large enough to hold all ingredients (12" diameter) and add the lemon zest and asparagus pieces. Sauté on medium heat until asparagus are hot, then add the stock and toss in the pasta and raise heat to high.

3. When pasta is steaming hot, swirl in the remaining butter, the lemon juice, and salt and pepper to taste. Serve in bowls sprinkled with Parmesan.

Light and Creamy Green Linguine

▶ SERVES 2

1 (14-ounce) package extra-firm tofu

½ cup lemon juice

1 cup spinach

2 cups cooked and rinsed gluten-free spinach linguine

1 cup nonfat Greek-style yogurt or soy yogurt

1 teaspoon all-natural sea salt

1 teaspoon freshly ground black pepper

1 teaspoon garlic powder

1. In a large skillet, sauté the tofu in 2 tablespoons of the lemon juice until slightly golden and crispy.

2. Add the spinach to the skillet and toss until wilted, about 1 minute. Remove from heat.

3. Toss the pasta with the tofu and spinach in the skillet and add the remaining lemon juice and yogurt; toss to combine thoroughly.

4. Season with the salt, pepper, and garlic powder.

GLUTEN-FREE PASTA VARIETIES

Now in your own grocery store, gluten-free pastas are widely available. In a variety of types like shells, rotini, spaghetti, and linguine, and even flavored with spinach, tomato, garlic, or basil by adding those specific ingredients to the pasta in the manufacturing process, gluten-free pastas are simple to create and make for a perfect gluten-free substitution that doesn't change the rest of your favorite recipes. You can enjoy gluten-free pasta for whichever dish you choose any night of the week, simply and easily.

Simple Spaghetti with Sautéed Tofu and Onions

▶ SERVES 2

1 medium Vidalia onion, peeled and sliced

3 tablespoons extra-virgin olive oil, divided

1 (14-ounce) package extra-firm tofu

2 tablespoons balsamic vinegar

2 cups cooked 100% whole-wheat spaghetti

1 teaspoon all-natural sea salt

1 teaspoon freshly ground black pepper

1 teaspoon garlic powder

1. In a large skillet over medium heat, sauté the onions in 1 tablespoon olive oil until slightly softened, about 4–6 minutes.

2. Add the tofu and balsamic to the skillet and sauté until tofu is browned and slightly crisp, about 6–8 minutes.

3. Add the spaghetti to the skillet and toss to combine; drizzle with the remaining olive oil until coated. Remove from heat and season with the salt, pepper, and garlic powder.

Veggie-Stuffed Shells

▶ SERVES 4

1 tablespoon extra-virgin olive oil

1 medium yellow onion, peeled and chopped

1 cup chopped red pepper

1 cup chopped broccoli

1 cup chopped zucchini

1 garlic clove, peeled and chopped

1 cup chopped spinach

2 cups cottage cheese or vegan cottage cheese

¼ cup ground flaxseed

8 ounces crumbled goat cheese or vegan soft cheese

1 teaspoon garlic powder

1 teaspoon all-natural sea salt

1 teaspoon freshly ground black pepper

12 cooked 100% whole-wheat pasta shells

THERE'S FLAXSEED IN THIS?!

When it comes to nutritious ingredients, some aren't always tempting to eat by the spoonful. Flaxseed can be a difficult ingredient to just add to a recipe as a topping or a garnish. One of the best ways to sneak some added essential flaxseed nutrients in your favorite foods is to add ground flaxseed to your favorite recipes in the cooking process. Acting as a thickening agent, and adding a slight nutty flavor, flaxseed additions just need careful attention to ensure that recipes remain as tasty and textured as intended.

1. Preheat oven to 350°F and prepare a 9" × 9" dish with olive oil spray.

2. In a skillet over medium heat, heat the olive oil and sauté the onion, red pepper, broccoli, zucchini, and chopped garlic until slightly softened but still crisp. Remove from heat and allow to cool 5 minutes.

3. In a large bowl, mix together the sautéed vegetables, spinach, cottage cheese, ground flaxseed, and goat cheese until thoroughly combined. Add garlic powder, sea salt, and pepper and stir to combine.

4. Place the shells into the prepared dish seam-side up and stuff each shell full of the sautéed vegetable mixture.

5. Cover the dish and bake 30–35 minutes. Remove cover and continue to bake 10–15 minutes or until shells are firm and stuffing is bubbly.

"Meat" Sauce Stuffed Shells

SERVES 2

1 cup minced yellow onion
2 cups vegan "meat" crumbles
1 tablespoon extra-virgin olive oil
2 cups tomato sauce, divided
2 cups cottage cheese or vegan cottage cheese
¼ cup ground flaxseed
1 teaspoon all-natural sea salt
1 teaspoon freshly ground black pepper
1 teaspoon garlic powder
6 cooked 100% whole-wheat shells

1. Preheat oven to 350°F and prepare a 9" × 9" glass pan with olive oil spray.

2. In a large skillet over medium heat, sauté the yellow onion and meat crumbles in the tablespoon of oil until onions are soft and crumbles are crispy.

3. Add 1 cup tomato sauce to the skillet and combine well. Remove from heat, add the cottage cheese and flaxseed, and mix well. Add salt, pepper, and garlic powder.

4. Place the shells in the prepared glass dish seam-side up and pack with the prepared mixture. Pour remaining cup of tomato sauce over top and bake uncovered 30–35 minutes.

Linguine with Leeks, Artichokes, and Garlic

▶ SERVES 2

2 cups (about 3 large) chopped leeks
2 cups chopped artichoke hearts
2 cloves garlic, peeled and minced
3 tablespoons extra-virgin olive oil, divided
2 cups cooked 100% whole-wheat linguine
2 teaspoons all-natural sea salt
1 teaspoon freshly ground black pepper

1. In a large skillet over medium heat, sauté the leeks, artichokes, and garlic in 1 tablespoon of the olive oil until slightly softened, about 4–5 minutes.
2. Add the linguine to the skillet and toss. Drizzle remaining olive oil over the linguine while combining to coat evenly.
3. Add salt and pepper.

Pesto and Pine Nut Penne

▶ SERVES 2

2 cups pesto
1 cup toasted pine nuts
4 ounces crumbled goat cheese or vegan soft cheese
3 cups cooked 100% whole-wheat penne pasta
¼ cup chopped fresh basil

1. In a large bowl, combine the pesto, pine nuts, and goat cheese until well-blended.
2. Add the penne to the pesto, pine nuts, and goat cheese and toss until evenly coated.
3. Plate two even servings and garnish with the chopped basil.

Sweet and Savory Pepper Penne

▶ SERVES 2

1 medium yellow onion, peeled and sliced

2 cloves garlic, peeled and minced

1 medium yellow bell pepper, seeded and sliced

1 medium red bell pepper, seeded and sliced

1 medium orange bell pepper, seeded and sliced

3 tablespoons extra-virgin olive oil, divided

1 tablespoon balsamic vinegar

2 cups cooked 100% whole-wheat penne

1 teaspoon all-natural sea salt

1 teaspoon freshly ground black pepper

1. In a large skillet over medium heat, sauté the onion, garlic, and peppers in 1 tablespoon of the oil until slightly softened and still crisp, about 4–6 minutes.

2. Add the balsamic vinegar to the skillet and toss to coat peppers and onions.

3. Add the penne to the skillet; drizzle remaining olive oil over penne and vegetables until evenly coated. Season with salt and pepper.

Ziti with Peppers and Marinated Mozzarella

▶ SERVES 4

1 pound fresh mozzarella cheese or smoked fresh mozzarella, cut into ½" cubes

3 tablespoons olive oil, divided

½ cup mixed chopped fresh herbs, such as parsley, chives, oregano, mint, etc.

Pinch of crushed red pepper

1 teaspoon red or white wine vinegar

Kosher salt and freshly ground black pepper to taste

1 tablespoon chopped garlic (about 3 cloves)

2 cups sliced onions

3 cups sliced mixed bell peppers

2 cups tomato sauce

8 ounces cooked (al dente) ziti

1 tablespoon unsalted butter

¼ cup grated Parmesan cheese

1. In a medium bowl, combine the mozzarella, 1 tablespoon of olive oil, the herbs, red pepper, vinegar, salt, and black pepper. Marinate at room temperature 30 minutes.

2. In a small bowl, combine remaining oil with chopped garlic. Heat a large skillet over high heat and bring a pot of water to a boil to reheat the pasta. Add the garlic oil to the pan, sizzle 10 seconds until the garlic turns white, and add the onions and peppers. Cook, stirring occasionally, until the onions are translucent, about 3 minutes. Add the tomato sauce and lower heat to a simmer.

3. Dip the pasta in boiling water to reheat; transfer hot pasta to the sauce, allowing some of the pasta water to drip into the sauce and thin it. Season to taste with salt and pepper. Remove from heat.

4. Toss with marinated mozzarella, butter, and Parmesan.

Quick Pasta Pesto

▶ SERVES 4

8 ounces ziti pasta
2 tablespoons olive oil
1 medium onion, peeled and thinly sliced
2 cups frozen peas
Salt and freshly ground black pepper to taste
⅓ cup pesto
1 cup chopped tomatoes
Butter and grated Parmesan cheese (optional)

1. Bring a large pot of water to boil over high heat and stir in the ziti. Cook according to package directions.

2. In the meantime, heat the olive oil in a large skillet over very high heat; add the onions and peas. When onions are translucent (3 minutes), use a slotted spoon or strainer to scoop the cooked pasta from the boiling water into the pan with the vegetables, allowing some of the pasta water to fall into the skillet along with it. Season well with salt and pepper.

3. Remove pan from the heat; add the pesto, chopped tomatoes, and butter and cheese if using. Toss to coat. Serve immediately.

Fettuccine Alfredo

▶ SERVES 4

8 ounces fettuccine

½ cup butter

2 cloves garlic, peeled and minced

1 tablespoon flour

1½ cups whole milk

2 tablespoons cream cheese

1 cup grated Parmesan cheese plus extra for garnish

Salt and freshly ground black pepper to taste

1. Prepare the pasta according to package directions. Drain and keep warm.

2. In a large saucepan over medium heat, melt the butter; add garlic and cook 2 minutes. Stir in the flour, then add the milk all at once, cooking and stirring over medium heat until thick and bubbly.

3. Add the cream cheese; stir until blended. Add the Parmesan cheese; continue cooking until all cheese has melted.

4. Toss with fettuccine; season with salt and pepper. Serve with extra Parmesan passed on the side.

PRECOOKING PASTA

Restaurant chefs have developed a trick for making pasta ready-to-serve in a minute, but still pleasingly al dente. The key is to just parboil it for less than 4 minutes, drain it, rinse it well in cold water, and toss it with a few drops of olive oil. It will not seem cooked when you drain it, but it will soften to the chewy consistency of fresh pasta as it sits. This can be done anywhere from an hour to a day before service. When you're ready to serve it, dip it for 1 minute in boiling water and toss with sauce of your choice. This works best with small dried pasta shapes like penne, ziti, rigatoni, shells, or farfalle (bow ties).

Linguine with Asparagus, Parmesan, and Cream

▶ SERVES 6

1 bunch asparagus (preferably chubby-stemmed)
2 teaspoons olive oil
2 medium shallots, peeled and thinly sliced
¼ cup white wine
¼ cup Vegetable Stock (see recipe in Chapter 5) or water
2 cups heavy cream
8 ounces linguine, cooked al dente, drained, tossed with a drop of olive oil
¼ cup Parmigiano-Reggiano cheese or other top-quality Parmesan
Juice of 1 medium lemon plus 6 lemon wedges
Kosher salt and freshly ground black pepper to taste

1. Trim the bottoms of the asparagus and use a vegetable peeler to peel off the skin from the bottom half of the stalks. Cut the asparagus into bite-sized (about 1") pieces. Heat the oil in a large skillet over medium heat; add the shallots and cook 3 minutes to soften them. Add the asparagus and wine; cook until the wine is mostly evaporated, then add the stock (or water).

2. When the asparagus are mostly cooked and the stock is mostly steamed out, stir in the cream and bring to a boil; add the linguine. Cook until the linguine is hot and the sauce is slightly thick; add the Parmigiano-Reggiano and remove from the heat.

3. Season with lemon juice, salt, and pepper. If necessary, adjust consistency with additional stock or water. Serve with lemon wedges on the side.

Orecchiette with Roasted Peppers, Green Beans, and Pesto

▶ SERVES 6

8 ounces orecchiette or other pasta shape
1 tablespoon olive oil
2 teaspoons chopped garlic
1 cup sliced roasted peppers
¼ pound green beans, blanched
¾ cup homemade pesto or fresh store-bought pesto, divided
¼ cup roughly chopped fresh Italian parsley
Salt and freshly ground black pepper to taste
1 tablespoon unsalted butter
Parmesan cheese for garnish
Lemon wedges for garnish

1. Bring a pot of salted water to boil; cook the pasta until al dente (still a little chewy), drain it, but save 1 cup of the cooking water for later. In a large mixing bowl, toss the pasta with a drop of olive oil; set aside.

2. In a small bowl, combine the olive oil and chopped garlic. Heat a large skillet 1 minute over medium heat. Add the garlic oil; sizzle 15 seconds, then add the roasted peppers and green beans. Sauté 3 minutes. Add ½ cup pesto; stir.

3. Add the cooked pasta, parsley, salt and pepper, and butter; simmer until heated through, adding a few drops of the reserved pasta water to make it saucy.

4. Remove from heat; toss with Parmesan cheese. Serve with lemon wedges and a little extra pesto on the side.

EGGS AND DAIRY

Cheese Soufflé

SERVES 6

¹⁄₂ cup unsalted butter
¹⁄₂ cup flour
¹⁄₂ teaspoon table salt
¹⁄₂ teaspoon paprika
Pinch of cayenne pepper or dash of hot sauce
2 cups milk
¹⁄₂ pound diced sharp Cheddar cheese
8 large eggs, separated

1. Preheat oven to 375°F. Butter a 10" soufflé dish and coat the inside with flour. Melt ½ cup butter in a double boiler or a steel bowl set over a pot of simmering water. Add the flour, salt, paprika, and cayenne (or pepper sauce); mix well. Gradually stir in the milk with a stiff whisk or wooden spoon. Cook, stirring constantly, until the mixture has become very thick. Stir in the cheese and continue stirring until all cheese is melted. Remove from the heat.

2. In a medium bowl, beat the yolks until they are lemon-colored, then gradually stir them into the cheese sauce. In a very clean bowl, whip the egg whites until they are stiff but not dry. Gently fold them into the cheese sauce and then pour this batter into the soufflé dish. At this point, the soufflé may be covered and refrigerated up to 1 hour or baked right away.

3. Bake 10 minutes. Reduce heat to 300°F and bake 25 minutes more. Serve immediately.

Artichoke and Cheese Squares

▶ SERVES 8

1 (12-ounce) jar marinated artichoke hearts, drained and liquid reserved
1 small onion, peeled and finely chopped
2 cloves garlic, peeled and finely minced
4 large eggs, beaten
2 tablespoons flour
½ teaspoon salt
¼ teaspoon freshly ground black pepper
¼ teaspoon dried oregano
¼ teaspoon Tabasco sauce
8 ounces shredded Monterey jack cheese
2 tablespoons chopped fresh parsley

1. Preheat oven to 325°F. Chop artichokes and set aside. Heat the marinade liquid in a medium skillet and sauté the onion and garlic in it until translucent, about 5 minutes.

2. In a mixing bowl, combine eggs, flour, salt, pepper, oregano, and Tabasco. Thoroughly mix in cheese, parsley, artichokes, and onion mixture.

3. Turn into a 7" × 11" baking dish. Bake 30 minutes until set. Cool to room temperature, cut into squares, and serve or reheat at 325°F 10 minutes.

Huevos Rancheros

SERVES 4

1 can Mexican-style black beans in sauce

2 cups Rancheros Salsa (see recipe in Chapter 3)

8 large eggs

½ cup half-and-half

½ teaspoon salt

2 tablespoons unsalted butter

8 (8" diameter) soft corn tortillas

1 cup shredded Monterey jack or mild Cheddar cheese

½ cup sour cream or tofu sour cream

Chopped cilantro

1. Heat the beans and salsa in separate pots over low heat. In a small bowl, scramble together the eggs, half-and-half, and salt. Melt the butter in a nonstick pan; cook the scrambled eggs over low heat until soft and creamy with small curds.

2. Soften the tortillas either by steaming or flash cooking over an open gas burner. Place 2 tortillas onto each plate. Divide the hot black beans evenly onto these tortillas. Spoon the eggs onto the beans, then sauce with a ladleful of Rancheros Salsa. Garnish with cheese, sour cream, and cilantro. Serve immediately.

Roasted Vegetable Frittata

▶ SERVES 8

1 medium zucchini, quartered lengthwise

1 medium yellow squash, quartered lengthwise

1 cup small white mushrooms

1 small (Italian) eggplant or ¼ of a regular eggplant, cut into large chunks

2 tablespoons olive oil

9 large eggs, beaten

¾ cup half-and-half

½ teaspoon salt

2 tablespoons unsalted butter

1 large baked potato, diced

1 medium onion, peeled and chopped

2 tablespoons chopped fresh Italian parsley or cilantro

1 cup shredded cheese (Monterey jack, Cheddar, or Havarti, for example)

½ cup diced tomatoes (about 1 large)

Freshly ground black pepper to taste

1. Preheat oven to 400°F. In a large bowl, toss zucchini, yellow squash, mushrooms, and eggplant with olive oil; spread onto a baking sheet or in a roasting pan. Roast until tender, about 20 minutes (note: this step can be done up to two days in advance). Raise oven temperature to 450°F.

2. In a bowl, whisk together the eggs, half-and-half, and salt. In an ovensafe 10" nonstick skillet, melt the butter over medium heat. Add the potatoes, onions, and parsley (or cilantro); cook until the onions are softened and the potatoes are slightly browned. Add the roasted vegetables and the egg mixture. Cook, stirring with a wooden spoon, until the mixture begins to thicken but is still mostly liquid. Stir in the cheese and tomatoes. Season with pepper. Place pan on center rack of oven and bake until frittata puffs slightly and begins to brown on top, about 15 minutes. Remove from oven and transfer frittata to a serving plate. Allow it to rest 5 minutes before cutting into eight wedges and serving, garnished with additional parsley or cilantro.

Spinach Quiche

▶ SERVES 6

1 batch Basic Pie Dough (see recipe in Chapter 11) or 1 store-bought
   unsweetened 9" pie shell
¼ cup chopped scallions
2 tablespoons unsalted butter
1 pound (1 package) fresh spinach, washed, stems removed, roughly
   chopped
Pinch of ground nutmeg
½ teaspoon salt
¼ teaspoon freshly ground black pepper
3 large eggs
6 ounces half-and-half or milk
¼ cup shredded Gruyère or Swiss cheese

1. Preheat oven to 350°F. If using fresh pie dough, roll out a disk 11" in
   diameter and line it into an ungreased 9" pie pan. Crimp edges, gently
   place wax paper over the unbaked crust, and fill the cavity with dried
   beans or pie beads. Bake until golden brown, 15–20 minutes. (This is
   known as "blind baking" the crust.) Cool on a rack; remove beans. If
   using a store-bought shell, bake according to package directions for
   "blind baking." Increase oven temperature to 375°F.

2. Heat the scallions and butter in a medium skillet over medium heat
   until they sizzle. Add spinach, nutmeg, salt, and pepper; cook until
   spinach is wilted, about 1–2 minutes. Whisk together eggs and half-
   and-half in a medium bowl. Add the spinach mixture. Sprinkle half of
   the cheese into the prebaked pie crust; add the spinach-egg mixture.
   Top with remaining cheese; bake 35 minutes until the top is domed
   and beginning to brown.

Creamed Carrots

SERVES 4

1 pound carrots, peeled, quartered lengthwise, cut into 2" sticks
½ cup water
2 tablespoons unsalted butter
½ teaspoon salt
1½ teaspoons sugar
½ cup light cream
Pinch of grated or ground nutmeg
White pepper (optional)

Combine the carrots, water, butter, salt, and sugar in a large skillet. Simmer over medium heat until most of the water has evaporated and the carrots are tender. Add the cream; simmer until it lightly coats the carrots and has a saucy consistency. Season carrots with nutmeg and white pepper if desired.

Stuffed Eggs

SERVES 8

8 large hard-boiled eggs
¼ cup Dijon mustard
3 tablespoons heavy cream
2 tablespoons finely chopped shallot
1 tablespoon rice wine vinegar
1 tablespoon chopped fresh chives
1 tablespoon chopped fresh tarragon
Salt and white pepper to taste
Unsalted butter

1. Preheat the broiler. Peel and halve the eggs. Take out the yolks and combine them with the mustard, cream, shallot, vinegar, chives, and tarragon in a medium bowl. Season with salt and white pepper. Transfer mixture to a piping bag and pipe it into the egg whites (you could also use a spoon).

2. Place the filled eggs in a baking dish or broiler pan. Dot the tops with a tiny nugget of butter and broil them until lightly browned, about 5 minutes. Serve warm.

Creamed Corn

6 ears sweet corn, shucked
1 tablespoon butter
¼ cup finely chopped shallots or onions
½ cup heavy cream
Salt and freshly ground black pepper
Freshly chopped chives (optional)

Using a knife, cut the kernels from the cob with a tip-to-stem slicing motion. You should have about 3 cups. Melt the butter in a large skillet over medium heat; add the shallots and cook until soft, about 3 minutes. Add the corn and cream and cook until thickened, about 2 minutes; season with salt and pepper. Garnish with chives if desired.

Chinese Soy Sauce Eggs

▶ SERVES 4

8 large eggs
½ cup soy sauce
2 tablespoons sugar
2 tablespoons Chinese five-spice powder (available in supermarkets)
1 tablespoon chopped garlic

Hard-boil the eggs in a large pot of boiling water about 10 minutes; drain, run them under cold water, and peel them. Bring 4 cups water to a boil in a medium saucepan. Add the soy sauce and sugar. Simmer 5 minutes; add the five-spice powder, garlic, and peeled eggs. Cover; simmer slowly at least 1 hour until the soy sauce's color has penetrated well into the eggs, all the way to the yolk. Cool in the cooking liquid and serve warm or room temperature.

Corn and Pepper Pudding

SERVES 6

2 tablespoons unsalted butter, melted

3 cups cubed bread, about ½" dice

3 medium poblano or small bell peppers, roasted, peeled, and diced

6 ears sweet corn, shucked, kernels cut off with a knife (about 3 cups)

¼ cup chopped chives

1 teaspoon salt

½ teaspoon freshly ground black pepper

4 large eggs

2 cups milk

¾ cup shredded jalapeño pepper jack cheese

1. Preheat oven to 350°F. In a medium bowl, combine the melted butter and bread cubes; turn bread out onto a baking sheet in a single layer and bake until lightly browned, about 10 minutes. In a mixing bowl, combine the roasted peppers, corn, chives, bread cubes, salt, and pepper. Transfer to a buttered 8" × 11" baking dish.

2. In a medium bowl, whisk together the eggs and milk; pour over bread mixture. Allow to sit 10 minutes to let the bread absorb the custard; top with the shredded cheese. Bake until set in the center and lightly browned on top, about 1 hour.

Scrambled Egg Burritos

▶ SERVES 4

1 tablespoon unsalted butter
1 medium onion, peeled and finely chopped (about 1 cup)
½ cup sliced roasted peppers
9 extra-large eggs, beaten
½ cup half-and-half
Few dashes of hot pepper sauce
2 cups shredded jalapeño jack cheese
Salt and freshly ground black pepper to taste
4 (12") flour tortillas
Salsa Fresca (see recipe in Chapter 3) or store-bought salsa

1. In a large skillet over medium heat, melt the butter; add the onions
   and sliced roasted peppers. Cook until the onions are soft and
   translucent, about 5 minutes. In a medium bowl, combine the eggs
   and half-and-half and then add them to the pan. Cook, stirring
   constantly with a wooden spoon, until the eggs are about half
   cooked—still very runny; add the hot pepper sauce, cheese, salt, and
   pepper. Remove from heat. Eggs should be soft, creamy, and have
   small curds.

2. Soften the tortillas by placing them directly atop the stove burner on
   medium heat; a few black spots are okay. Spoon ¼ of the egg mixture
   slightly off center on one of the tortillas. Fold the sides in upon the
   egg and roll the tortilla away from yourself, folding the filling in
   and tucking with your fingers to keep even pressure. Repeat with
   remaining tortillas. Serve with salsa.

Miso Eggs Benedict

▶ SERVES 4

3 tablespoons white vinegar
1 teaspoon salt
4 extra-large eggs
2 English muffins, split
4 tablespoons butter
½ teaspoon miso paste
½ cup homemade or store-bought hollandaise sauce
Chives (optional)
Hot pepper sauce (optional)

1. Combine the vinegar and salt in a deep skillet with 2" of water; bring to a boil over high heat. Crack each egg into its own cup. When water boils, lower heat as low as you can. Gently lower the eggs into the hot water one by one and pour them from the cups into the pan. Set the muffins to toast.

2. Poach the eggs no more than 3 minutes, then remove them with a slotted spoon allowing excess water to drain back into the skillet. Transfer poached eggs to a waiting plate. In a small bowl, mash together the butter and miso; spread this mixture onto the toasted muffins. Place one poached egg onto each. Spoon generous helpings of hollandaise sauce onto each and serve immediately with a sprinkling of chives and hot pepper sauce on the side. Note: Eggs can be poached up to a day in advance and stored submerged in cold water. To reheat, gently place in fresh boiling water for 1 minute before using.

Fricos (Cheese Crisps)

▶ SERVES 4

1 cup finely shredded Parmigiano-Reggiano or other cheese

Heat a nonstick skillet over medium heat. Sprinkle 1 tablespoon cheese into a small mound on the pan. Cook until the bottom is nicely browned, then transfer to drain on paper towels. Repeat with remaining cheese. They are soft and oozy and require a little practice to handle them properly, so have a little extra cheese ready in case the first few are less than perfect.

Crepes

▶ MAKES ABOUT 8 CREPES

½ cup flour	1 tablespoon olive oil
3 large eggs	¼ teaspoon kosher salt
1 cup milk	Butter

1. In a medium bowl, whisk together the flour and eggs until they form a smooth paste. Gradually whisk in the milk, olive oil, and salt.

2. Heat a 10" nonstick skillet over medium heat. Add some butter and spread it around the pan with a brush or the corner of a towel. Add ¼ cup batter to the pan. Swirl the pan around in a circular pattern to evenly distribute the batter.

3. Cook undisturbed until the edges become visibly brown. Using a wooden or rubber spatula, lift the edge of the crepe from the pan. Quickly flip the crepe using your fingers or a wooden spoon. Cook 30 seconds on the second side, then slide onto a plate; keep warm while you repeat the procedure with remaining batter. Crepes can be stacked one atop the other for storage.

Boursin Omelet

3 large eggs

¼ cup half-and-half or milk

¼ teaspoon salt

Pinch of white pepper or a dash of hot pepper sauce

1 teaspoon unsalted butter

2 tablespoons Boursin or other creamy, tangy cheese, such as goat cheese

1 teaspoon chopped fresh chives or scallions

1. In a medium bowl, whisk together the eggs, half-and-half, salt, and pepper (or hot pepper sauce). Melt the butter in an 8" nonstick skillet over medium-low heat (this is a case where a truly nonstick skillet is really important). Swirl the pan to thoroughly coat it with butter; add the egg mixture. Allow the eggs to sizzle for a minute without disturbing them. Then, using a wooden implement or heatproof rubber spatula, scramble the still-liquidy eggs around in the pan; smooth out the top with your implement and allow to cook undisturbed until the eggs are 90 percent set but still glistening on top (residual heat will cook the egg the rest of the way when you fold it).

2. Crumble the cheese into the center of the omelet. Now, you have to make a choice: cigar-shaped or the easy way.

For a cigar-shaped ("French rolled") omelet:

1. Strike the handle of the pan with the heel of your hand to loosen the omelet and move it to the tip of the pan; use an implement to fold the third of the omelet closest to you into the center, covering the cheese.

2. Place a plate at a 90-degree angle to the tip of the pan.

3. Gently tilt the pan to the plate, allowing the omelet to "roll" into a perfect cigar shape directly in the center of the plate.

4. Sprinkle with chives.

For a simple omelet:

Use an implement to fold the omelet in half, slide onto the plate, sprinkle with chives, and enjoy.

Cottage Cheese Blintzes

▶ SERVES 4

1 cup cottage cheese
½ cup ricotta
2 tablespoons sugar
1 large egg yolk
12 Crepes (see recipe in this chapter)
2 tablespoons melted unsalted butter
Confectioners' sugar for dusting
Jams and preserves

1. In a blender or food processor, pulse the cottage cheese, ricotta, and sugar until smooth. Transfer to a bowl; whisk in the yolk.

2. Preheat oven to 325°F. Butter a 9" × 13" baking dish. On a clean work surface, spoon a generous tablespoon of cheese filling onto the bottom third of a crepe. Fold in the sides and fold the bottom up to envelop the filling; roll the crepe away from yourself. Repeat with remaining crepes; line them into the baking dish and brush them with the melted butter. Bake 10–15 minutes until they have become visibly plump. Serve with a dusting of confectioners' sugar and assorted jams and preserves on the side.

Tomato and Cheese Tart

▶ SERVES 4-6

8 ounces store-bought (or homemade) puff pastry, thawed

1 tablespoon olive oil

4 leeks, thoroughly washed and sliced

3 sprigs (about 2 teaspoons) fresh thyme leaves, picked, or a scant teaspoon dried

Kosher salt and freshly ground black pepper

6 ounces raclette or other semisoft cheese, such as Havarti or Gouda, sliced

2–3 medium tomatoes, thinly sliced

Pinch of sugar

1. Preheat oven to 375°F. Roll the pastry out to fit a 14" × 4" oblong rectangular tart pan (you can also use a 10" circular tart pan—adjust dough dimensions accordingly); prick the rolled dough with the tines of a fork in several places. Arrange the dough in the pan and refrigerate until ready to use.

2. Heat the olive oil in a medium skillet over moderate heat; sauté the leeks and thyme until the leeks are soft and translucent, about 5 minutes. Season with salt and pepper; remove from heat and cool to room temperature. Spoon the leeks into the tart shell; cover with the cheese. Arrange the tomatoes in rows or concentric circles (depending on what type of pan you're using) and sprinkle them with a little sugar. Bake 40–45 minutes until cheese begins to brown and the crust is golden.

Brie Timbales with Roasted Red Pepper Sauce

▶ SERVES 8

4 teaspoons melted butter
7 ounces Brie
6 ounces cream cheese
4 ounces sour cream
3 large eggs
Pinch of cayenne pepper
Salt to taste
White pepper or hot pepper sauce to taste
1 teaspoon butter
1 recipe Roasted Red Bell Pepper Purée (see recipe in this chapter)

1. Preheat oven to 350°F. Bring 2 quarts water to a boil in a large pot. In a food processor or blender, combine the melted butter, Brie, cream cheese, sour cream, and eggs; process until very smooth. Season with cayenne, salt, and pepper (or pepper sauce).

2. Butter 8 (4-ounce) ramekins or custard cups (small teacups will do fine also); fill with egg mixture. Place into a deep roasting pan or baking dish; place in the oven and pour boiling water in until it reaches halfway up the sides of the cups. Bake until set, about 30 minutes. Allow the timbales to sit at room temperature 10–15 minutes. Loosen timbales by running a knife around the inside of the cup and then inverting the cups onto small plates. Spoon Roasted Red Bell Pepper Purée around.

Roasted Red Bell Pepper Purée

▶ SERVES 8

4 medium roasted red bell peppers, chopped
1 tablespoon tomato paste
Zest and juice of 1 lemon
2 tablespoons extra-virgin olive oil
Salt and freshly ground black pepper to taste

Combine all ingredients in a food processor or blender. Purée until smooth. Heat in a saucepan before serving.

Greek Salad Tacos

▶ SERVES 4

8 (6") corn tortillas
8 ounces feta, cut into 8 slices
2 cups shredded romaine or iceberg lettuce
8 thin slices ripe tomato
24 pitted kalamata olives
¼ cup extra-virgin olive oil
1 teaspoon dried oregano, preferably Mexican
Salt and freshly ground black pepper to taste

1. Soften the tortillas over a stove burner (a few black spots are okay).
2. Place a slice of feta in the center of one tortilla, along with a pinch of lettuce, a slice of tomato, and three olives. Repeat with remaining tortillas. In a bowl, whisk together the olive oil, oregano, salt, and pepper. Drizzle the tacos with spoonfuls of dressing and serve with remaining dressing on the side.

Ricotta and Goat Cheese Crespelle

SERVES 4

8 ounces ricotta, drained over cheesecloth or a fine strainer
4 ounces (one log) fresh goat cheese softened at room temperature
¼ cup roughly chopped fresh Italian parsley plus more for garnish
1 large egg, beaten
Salt and freshly ground black pepper to taste
8 Crepes (see recipe in this chapter)
2 cups tomato sauce

1. Preheat oven to 350°F. In a medium bowl, whisk together the ricotta, goat cheese, parsley, egg, salt, and pepper. Place 1½ tablespoons filling onto the bottom third of a crepe; roll away from yourself forming a filled cylinder. Repeat with remaining crepes. Line them up in a buttered 9" × 13" baking dish.

2. Bake 20 minutes until tops are slightly crisp. Warm tomato sauce and make ½-cup pools in the centers of four plates. Place two crespelle onto each plate. Garnish with additional chopped parsley if desired.

Noodle Pudding

SERVES 6

2 large eggs
¼ cup sugar
1 cup cottage cheese
½ cup sour cream
¼ teaspoon salt
¼ cup raisins, soaked for 15 minutes in 1 cup hot tap water
2 cups dried wide egg noodles
3 tablespoons butter at room temperature
Ground cinnamon

1. Preheat oven to 350°F. Combine eggs, sugar, cottage cheese, sour cream, salt, and raisins in a medium bowl; stir well. Cook noodles according to package directions; drain and toss with butter. Add noodles to cottage cheese mixture; toss to coat. Transfer to a buttered 9" square baking dish. Cover with foil.

2. Bake until fully set in the middle, about 45 minutes, uncovering halfway through. Dust with cinnamon and allow to rest 10 minutes before cutting into portions.

Cheese Fondue

▶ SERVES 6

1 garlic clove, halved

2 cups dry white wine

¾ pound (3 cups) shredded Emmental (Swiss) cheese

¾ pound (3 cups) shredded Gruyère cheese

1 tablespoon cornstarch

2 tablespoons kirsch

Assorted steamed vegetables such as carrot sticks, broccoli, cauliflower, and green beans

Cubes of French bread

1. Rub the inside of a medium saucepan with the cut side of the garlic. Discard the clove or leave it in. Add the wine and cook over medium heat until it simmers. Whisk in the cheese in small handfuls, making sure that the last addition has completely melted before adding the next. Combine the cornstarch and kirsch into a paste; whisk into cheese mixture. Simmer the fondue gently 5–7 minutes to allow the cornstarch to thicken.

2. Transfer the cheese mixture to a fondue pot and set a low flame under it—just enough to keep it at the border of simmering. Assemble a platter with the vegetables and bread cubes, and set the table with either long fondue forks or long wooden skewers.

Scrambled Eggs Masala

SERVES 2

2 tablespoons butter
¼ cup chopped onion
¼ teaspoon cumin seed, toasted in a dry pan and crushed (or very fresh ground cumin, toasted a minute in a dry pan)

¼ cup diced tomato
4 large eggs, beaten
Salt and white pepper to taste
4 teaspoons chopped fresh mint leaves

1. Melt the butter in a medium nonstick skillet over medium heat. Add the onions; cook 5–8 minutes until soft. Add cumin and tomatoes; cook 1 minute more.

2. Stir in the eggs, salt, and pepper. Using a wooden spoon, constantly stir the eggs until they form soft, creamy curds; transfer to plates and serve immediately. Garnish with the mint.

Baked Pasta Custard

SERVES 4–6

4 large eggs
1 cup part-skim or whole-milk ricotta cheese
1 cup confectioners' sugar
2 cups cooked orzo
½ cup slivered almonds

½ cup heavy cream
1 tablespoon lemon zest
2 teaspoons vanilla extract
1 teaspoon lemon extract
Lemon curd for garnish (optional)

1. Preheat oven to 350°F. Lightly butter a 2-quart baking dish and set aside.

2. In a large bowl, beat the eggs until light and foamy. Beat in the ricotta cheese and sugar. Fold in the orzo, almonds, cream, lemon zest, vanilla extract, and lemon extract and stir until well combined.

3. Pour mixture into prepared baking dish and bake about 1 hour or until the custard browns and the center is firm. Garnish with a dollop of lemon curd. Serve hot or at room temperature.

Hawaiian Turnovers

▶ SERVES 8

1 (8-ounce) package cream cheese at room temperature
½ cup confectioners' sugar
½ cup crushed pineapple, very well drained
½ cup shredded coconut
½ cup sliced almonds
1 teaspoon vanilla extract
½ teaspoon salt
1 (16.3-ounce) package jumbo buttermilk refrigerator biscuits
Milk for brushing

1. Preheat oven to 350°F. Spray a nonstick baking sheet with nonstick cooking spray.

2. In a large mixing bowl, beat the cream cheese and sugar together until smooth and slightly fluffy. Fold in the pineapple, coconut, almonds, vanilla, and salt.

3. Unfold the biscuit circles one at a time. Roll them out on a lightly floured surface to about 5½" round. Put about 2 tablespoons of the filling mixture into the center of the circle and fold one side over the filling to the other side. Crimp the edges shut and brush the top with milk. Place on the baking sheet. Repeat with the remaining ingredients.

4. Bake about 15 minutes or until the turnovers turn golden. Remove from the oven and eat hot or set aside for later use.

Fruit-and-Cheese Quesadillas

▶ SERVES 4

4 tablespoons strawberry jam
4 (6"–8") whole-wheat flour tortillas
2 cups shredded mozzarella cheese
1 cup diced fresh strawberries plus extra for sprinkling
4 tablespoons strawberry yogurt for garnish
Confectioners' sugar for dusting

1. Spread 1 tablespoon jam on a tortilla and sprinkle it with ¼ cup mozzarella cheese and ¼ cup diced strawberries. Fold over the tortilla to enclose the filling. Repeat with the remaining tortillas, jam, mozzarella, and strawberries.

2. Spray a medium skillet with nonstick cooking spray and heat it over medium heat. Cook the quesadillas one or two at a time until golden on the bottom, about 3 minutes. Flip over and cook the second side until golden and the cheese has melted.

3. Top each quesadilla with a dollop of yogurt, a sprinkling of strawberries, and a dusting of confectioners' sugar. Serve hot.

"Sausage" Bread Pudding

SERVES 4

1 tablespoon olive oil

1 teaspoon minced garlic

1 cup soy "sausage" meat

1 teaspoon Cajun or Creole seasoning or hot sauce to taste

2 cups whole milk

3 tablespoons melted butter

4 large eggs

2 cups shredded Cheddar or Monterey jack cheese

3 cups cubed sourdough bread

2 cups fresh blackberries or blueberries

SOY SAUSAGES

Made from soy proteins, soy "sausages" are available as links or as a compact product packed in a tube. In the tube, the soy meat is easy to crumble and sauté like its pork sausage counterpart; alternatively, it slices easily and pan-fries like a patty. Look for soy sausage products in a refrigerated case displayed with other vegetarian and vegan ingredients.

1. Preheat oven to 375°F. Lightly butter a 2-quart baking dish.

2. Heat the oil in a large skillet over medium heat and sauté the garlic about 30 seconds. Add and crumble the "sausage" meat, stirring as you crumble, and season with the Cajun seasoning. Reduce the heat to low.

3. Meanwhile, in a medium bowl, beat together the milk, butter, and eggs until foamy. Stir in the cheese and sausage mixture. Put the bread into the baking dish and pour the milk mixture over the bread.

4. Bake the custard about 45 minutes or until puffy and golden. Serve hot with the fruit topping.

DESSERTS

Tarte Tatin

▶ SERVES 8

8 tablespoons butter at room temperature

1 cup sugar

6 medium Gala or Golden Delicious apples, peeled, cored, and cut into
quarters

1 thin (⅛") sheet store-bought puff pastry, cut into a circle 12" in diameter

1. Preheat oven to 350°F. Spread the butter evenly into a 10" tarte tatin
mold or heavy 10" nonstick ovenproof skillet. Evenly spread sugar on
sides and bottom of the pan. Starting at the edge of the pan, arrange
apples peeled-side down in concentric circles, fitting apples closely
together.

2. Place pan over high heat and cook without stirring until sugar
caramelizes and turns dark golden brown, 15–20 minutes. Remove
from heat and gently press the apples closer together with a wooden
spoon, eliminating any gaps. Cover the apples with the puff pastry.
The dough will overlap the rim of the pan. Bake until pastry is golden
brown, about 30 minutes.

3. Remove from oven and rest it 5 minutes. Place a large serving plate on
top and rapidly invert the tart; remove the pan. Serve warm.

Chocolate Mousse

▶ SERVES 8

1 tablespoon vanilla extract plus a few drops, divided

6 ounces dark chocolate (bittersweet)

1½ cups heavy cream

2½ tablespoons confectioners' sugar

6 large egg whites, whipped to medium-soft peaks and refrigerated

Additional whipped cream and chocolate shavings for garnish (optional)

CHOCOLATE CURLS

Use a swivel vegetable peeler to make attractive shavings and curls from a block of chocolate. Just start with a large flat surface of chocolate, like the edge of a bar or the side of a hunk, and shave away from yourself, letting the curls fall onto whatever food you're garnishing. Don't try to pick them up with your fingers, though, because they melt faster than butter.

1. Chill 8 (8-ounce) wineglasses. Combine 1 tablespoon vanilla and chocolate in a double boiler (or a steel mixing bowl set over a pot of simmering water). Warm, stirring occasionally, until melted and smooth. In a medium bowl, whip together the cream, confectioners' sugar, and a few drops of vanilla until it forms soft peaks when the whisk is lifted from it.

2. Gently fold ⅓ of the whipped cream into the chocolate mixture. Fold the chocolate mixture back into the rest of the whipped cream, mixing only as much as is necessary to incorporate it most of the way (a few streaks of chocolate are okay). Fold the whipped egg whites very gently into the chocolate cream mixture just barely enough to incorporate. Fill the mousse into a pastry bag with a star tip (or a plastic bag with a corner cut out) and pipe it into the chilled wineglasses. Cover the glasses individually with plastic wrap and chill at least 6 hours until set. Garnish with a spoonful of whipped cream and chocolate shavings if desired.

Cinnamon-Apple Cobbler with Rome Beauty Apples

▶ SERVES 8

Filling
8 or 9 Rome Beauty apples, peeled, cored, and diced into 1" pieces
Pinch of salt
¼ teaspoon ground nutmeg
1 capful vanilla extract
1½ teaspoons ground cinnamon
½ cup sugar
¼ cup flour
Juice of ½ lemon

Biscuit Topping
3 cups flour
½ teaspoon salt
2 teaspoons baking powder
2 large eggs
½ cup sugar
⅔ cup milk
6 ounces melted butter

1. Make the filling: Preheat oven to 375°F. In a large bowl, mix together the apples, pinch salt, nutmeg, vanilla, cinnamon, ½ cup sugar, ¼ cup flour, and lemon juice. Place in a 6" × 10" baking dish.

2. Make the topping: In a large bowl, sift together the 3 cups flour, ½ teaspoon salt, and baking powder. In a separate bowl, combine the eggs, ½ cup sugar, milk, and melted butter.

3. Add the wet ingredients to the dry, mixing only until they are well combined. Do not overmix. Batter should have consistency of thick oatmeal. Adjust with milk if necessary.

4. Spread batter over fruit filling as evenly as possible with your hands. Some holes are natural and will make for a more attractive presentation.

5. Bake on bottom shelf of oven 90 minutes, turning halfway through and checking after 1 hour. Fruit should be bubbling thoroughly and biscuit topping should be nicely browned. Allow to cool at least 15 minutes before serving with vanilla ice cream and a sprig of fresh mint.

Pink McIntosh Applesauce with Cranberry Chutney

▶ SERVES 6

1 (2"-long) cinnamon stick
8 McIntosh and 2 Red Delicious apples, washed, cored, and quartered
¼ cup sugar
¼ cup water
1 recipe Cranberry Chutney (see recipe in this chapter)

1. Warm the cinnamon stick, dry, over medium heat in a heavy-bottomed pot large enough to hold all the apples. Reduce heat to low and add the apples, sugar, and water. Cover tightly.

2. Simmer gently 40 minutes, then uncover and simmer 10 minutes more.

3. Strain through a food mill or push through a strainer with a flexible spatula. Cool and serve with a dollop of Cranberry Chutney.

Old-Fashioned Baked Apples

4 large baking apples (Romes or
  Cortlands are good)

8 whole cloves

2 ounces (½ stick) butter

⅓ cup light brown sugar plus more for
  dusting

½ teaspoon ground cinnamon plus more
  for dusting

MICROWAVE OPTION

This dish works in the microwave oven, though the flavor develops better in the conventional oven. To microwave, follow steps 1 and 2, then score the apples 1" from the bottom, cover, and cook on high 5 minutes per apple.

1. Preheat oven to 350°F. Wash and dry apples thoroughly. Using a small knife, cut a divot from the top of the apples, leaving the stem intact. This "cover" will be replaced when baking. Scoop out the seeds and core with a melon baller or small spoon. Drop 2 cloves into each apple.

2. In a small bowl, knead together the butter, ⅓ cup brown sugar, and ½ teaspoon cinnamon until it is a paste. Divide equally over the scooped apples, leaving enough space to replace the tops.

3. Place apples in a baking dish with ½ cup of water on the bottom. Bake 1 hour. Sprinkle with brown sugar and cinnamon before serving.

Golden Delicious Apple Crisp

▶ SERVES 8

8 or 9 Golden Delicious apples, peeled, cored, and cut into 1" cubes
3 tablespoons granulated sugar
¼ teaspoon ground cloves
½ teaspoon ground cinnamon
Juice of ½ lemon
1 cup plus 2 tablespoons all-purpose flour, divided
1 cup almonds
1 cup light brown sugar
⅛ teaspoon salt
4 ounces (1 stick) unsalted butter, cold, cut into pea-sized pieces

1. Preheat oven to 350°F. In a large bowl, toss the apples with granulated sugar, spices, lemon juice, and 2 tablespoons flour. Pour mixture into a 6" × 10" baking dish.
2. Toast almonds on a baking sheet until golden brown, about 10–12 minutes. Cool then roughly chop.
3. In a medium bowl, use your hands to rub together 1 cup flour, brown sugar, salt, and butter until mixture clumps. Add chopped almonds and cover the fruit evenly with this topping. Bake on bottom shelf of oven 1 hour until fruit is bubbling and topping is crisp. Serve with vanilla whipped cream or vanilla ice cream.

Apple Walnut Upside-Down Pie

▶ SERVES 8

Caramel-Walnut Topping

1 cup light brown sugar
4 ounces (1 stick) unsalted butter
1 cup roughly chopped toasted walnut pieces
Pinch of salt

Pie Dough and Apple Filling

1 recipe Basic Pie Dough (see recipe in this chapter)
8 or 9 Granny Smith apples, peeled, cored, and diced into 1" slices
½ cup sugar (give or take, depending on sweetness of apples)
1½ teaspoons ground cinnamon
½ teaspoon ground allspice
¼ teaspoon ground cloves
¼ cup flour
Pinch of salt

1. For the caramel-walnut topping: Melt brown sugar and butter together in a heavy-bottomed skillet over medium-high heat until smooth and bubbling. Cook 5 minutes. Stir in walnuts and salt and remove from heat. Spread into bottom of 9" pie pan.

2. For pie dough and filling: Preheat oven to 375°F. Roll out bottom crust very thin (¼") and drape over caramel/walnut-lined pie pan. In a large bowl, mix filling ingredients and fill the pie, mounding somewhat in the center.

3. Roll out top crust (¼"). Brush rim of bottom crust with a little water to seal the crusts together and cover the pie loosely with the top. Crimp the edges. Make several vents using a fork or the tip of a knife.

4. Bake 1 hour until filling is bubbling. Cool, then reheat quickly in a hot oven before inverting and unmolding. Serve with cinnamon ice cream.

Basic Pie Dough

▶ MAKES ENOUGH DOUGH FOR 1 PIE

6 ounces (1½ sticks) unsalted butter, cold, cut into pea-sized pieces
2 cups flour (pastry flour is best, but you can use all-purpose)
½ teaspoon salt
½ cup very cold water

1. Place the diced butter in a medium bowl. Sift flour and salt together over the bowl. Using your hands, break up the butter into the flour until the flour assumes the color of the butter. There should still be some nuggets of unmixed butter.

2. Sprinkle in most of the water and work quickly with your hands until dough clumps together. Add extra water if the dough feels too dry to roll. Do not overmix. Separate dough into two balls, wrap separately, and refrigerate at least 30 minutes.

Cranberry Chutney

▶ SERVES 2 OR 3

2 cups fresh or frozen cranberries
¼ cup very finely diced red onion
1 cup sugar
6 whole cloves
¼ cup water

Combine all ingredients in a small heavy-bottomed saucepot. Simmer 10–15 minutes until all cranberries are broken and have a saucy consistency.

Tiramisu

▶ SERVES 12

1 cup quick-dissolving sugar

9 large eggs, separated

3 teaspoon vanilla extract

About 1½ pounds (750 grams) mascarpone (Italian cream cheese)

1 tablespoon sweet Marsala wine

3 cups cream, whipped to medium-soft peaks

2 cups espresso or very strong brewed coffee

2 tablespoons dark rum (such as Myers's Original Dark Rum)

1 package (about 60 pieces) ladyfingers (savoiardi)

Cocoa powder for dusting

Mint sprigs for garnish

> **MASCARPONE: IT AIN'T PHILLY**
>
> Italian cream cheese, known as mascarpone, is the key ingredient in the wildly popular dessert, tiramisu. It's also the perfect rich, creamy accompaniment to fresh figs, or August Georgia peaches. Think yogurt without the tang. It's smooth and unsalted. Buy it at specialty gourmet shops, Italian food stores, and the dairy sections of most modern supermarkets.

1. In a medium steel or glass bowl over a bath of warm water, stir together sugar, yolks, and vanilla until sugar dissolves. In a medium bowl with an electric mixer or by hand, combine the mascarpone and Marsala. Fold into the yolk mixture. Fold in the whipped cream.

2. In a medium bowl, combine the coffee and rum. Quickly dip ¾ of the ladyfingers into the coffee mixture and use them to line the bottom and sides of a 10" springform pan or deep cake pan. Pour half of the mascarpone mixture into the cookie-lined pan; dust thoroughly with cocoa powder. Dip remaining ladyfingers in coffee mixture and layer then into the pan. Top that with the remaining mascarpone mixture.

3. Cover with plastic wrap and refrigerate overnight. Dust top with cocoa powder before cutting into twelve portions with a hot, wet knife; serve garnished with mint sprigs.

Crème Caramel

▶ SERVES 8

1½ cups sugar, divided
½ cup water
3 cups heavy cream
6 large egg yolks
1 teaspoon vanilla extract

1. Preheat oven to 350°F. In a small heavy-bottomed skillet, combine ¾ cup sugar with ½ cup water. Bring to a boil over medium-high heat and cook until sugar caramelizes into a deep orange brown. Watch the sugar closely when it begins to color; swirl the pan to keep it evenly colored. Pour immediately from the pan into the bottoms of eight (6-ounce) custard cups or ramekins.

2. In a small saucepan over medium-high heat, bring cream and remaining ¾ cup sugar just to the boiling point; stir to dissolve the sugar. Place egg yolks in a medium bowl and pour the scalded cream mixture over them, whisking vigorously and constantly. Add vanilla and stir to combine. Ladle this cream mixture into the caramel-filled cups. Set the cups into a deep roasting pan or casserole dish and place on the center rack of the oven. Carefully pour water into the roasting pan to just past the cream and egg mixture in the cups. Bake exactly 50 minutes. Remove from oven to cool to room temperature, then refrigerate at least 8 hours or overnight.

3. To unmold the Crème Caramels, loosen the edges of the custard with a small knife, then invert the molds onto a plate.

Flourless Chocolate Cake

▶ SERVES 12

8 large eggs
1 pound semisweet chocolate
8 ounces (2 sticks) unsalted butter, cut into pieces the size of a hazelnut
¼ cup strong brewed coffee (optional)
Confectioners' sugar and/or cocoa powder for dusting

1. Preheat oven to 325°F. Grease an 8" or 9" springform pan and line the bottom with waxed paper. Wrap the outside of the pan in foil to prevent leaks. Prepare a pot of boiling water.

2. In a medium bowl using a handheld or standing electric mixer, beat the eggs until double in volume (about 1 quart), about 5 minutes. Melt the chocolate, butter, and coffee in a double boiler or in a medium bowl in the microwave until very smooth, stirring occasionally. Fold in the whipped eggs in three additions, mixing only enough as is necessary to incorporate them. Pour into prepared springform pan.

3. Place springform into a deep roasting pan and place on the lower middle rack of the oven. Pour enough boiling water into the roasting pan to come about halfway up the sides of the cake pan. Bake about 25 minutes until the cake rises slightly, has a thin, wispy crust, and reads 140°F on an instant-read thermometer inserted in the center. Transfer springform to a wire rack and cool to room temperature. Refrigerate overnight. Warm sides of springform with a hot, wet towel to loosen; then pop open, cut with a hot, wet knife, and serve dusted with confectioners' sugar and/or cocoa powder.

Sour Cream Butter Cake

▶ SERVES 12

4 large egg yolks
⅔ cup sour cream, divided
1½ teaspoons vanilla extract
2 cups sifted cake flour
1 cup sugar
½ teaspoon baking powder
½ teaspoon baking soda
½ teaspoon salt
6 ounces (1½ sticks) unsalted butter softened to room temperature

1. Preheat oven to 350°F. Grease a 9" cake pan, dust it with flour, and line the bottom with waxed paper. In a medium bowl, whisk together the yolks, ¼ of the sour cream, and the vanilla. In a large, separate bowl, mix the flour, sugar, baking powder, baking soda, and salt; whisk vigorously to combine.

2. Add the butter and remaining sour cream to the flour mixture and mix well until flour is completely moistened. Add the egg mixture to the flour mixture in three separate additions, mixing between each addition. Pour into prepared cake pan.

3. Bake in the middle of the oven until a toothpick inserted in the center comes out clean, usually about 35–40 minutes. Start checking at 25 minutes, since oven temperatures and ingredient characteristics vary, and it might be done quicker. Cool 10 minutes, then take out of pan and cool completely on a wire rack.

4. To frost, cut laterally in half and frost both sections, then stack, smooth sides, and refrigerate to set.

Blondies

1½ cups flour

½ teaspoon baking powder

½ teaspoon salt

6 ounces (1½ sticks) unsalted butter at room temperature

Generous 1¾ cups brown sugar

2 teaspoons vanilla extract

3 large eggs

6 ounces (about 1 cup) semisweet chocolate chunks or chips

1. Preheat oven to 350°F. Butter a 9" baking pan. In a medium bowl using a stiff wire whisk, whisk together the flour, baking powder, and salt. In a separate medium bowl, combine the butter, brown sugar, and vanilla and cream together using an electric mixer or by hand until light and fluffy (about 2 minutes). Gradually beat in the eggs, working each one in completely before adding the next. Scrape down mixing bowl; add the flour mixture. Beat just long enough to incorporate. Mix in chocolate chunks. Transfer the batter into the prepared baking pan and smooth with a spatula.

2. Bake until a toothpick inserted in the center comes out clean, about 30–35 minutes. Cool at room temperature at least 1 hour. Cut into 36 pieces. Will keep refrigerated 1 week or in freezer up to 6 weeks.

Pears Poached in White Wine with Strawberry Sauce

▶ SERVES 8

1 bottle (750 ml) white wine (Chardonnay or Riesling are both excellent for this)

Zest of 1 lemon, shaved off with a vegetable peeler in strips

8 whole cloves

2 whole cinnamon sticks

1 cup sugar, divided

4 Bosc pears, peeled, halved lengthwise, seeds scooped out

1 pint strawberries, hulled and halved

1 teaspoon vanilla extract

8 sprigs fresh mint

1. Combine the wine, lemon zest, cloves, cinnamon sticks, and ½ cup sugar in a large (4- to 5-quart) pot; bring to a boil. Reduce heat to a simmer and add the pears, arranging them so they are mostly submerged. Cover tightly and cook 5 minutes; remove from heat and leave to steep 20 minutes. Chill.

2. In a blender, combine the strawberries, remaining ½ cup sugar, and vanilla. Purée until smooth, adding a few drops of water if necessary to get things started.

3. Spoon the sauce onto dessert plates to form small pools midplate. Serve the pears cut-side down atop the sauce, garnished with mint sprigs at the stem end.

Chocolate Chip Cookies

▶ SERVES ABOUT 12

2½ cups all-purpose flour

1 teaspoon baking soda

1 teaspoon salt

1 cup (2 sticks) unsalted butter, softened

¾ cup sugar

¾ cup (packed) light brown sugar

1 teaspoon vanilla extract

2 large eggs

2 cups (12-ounce package) semisweet chocolate chips

1. Preheat oven to 375°F. In a mixing bowl, whisk together flour, baking soda, and salt. In a separate medium bowl, cream together the butter, granulated sugar, brown sugar, and vanilla using a wooden spoon. Add the eggs one at a time to the sugar mixture, mixing until incorporated before adding the next one.

2. Add the flour mixture in three additions, mixing just enough to incorporate after each addition. Stir in the chocolate chips. Drop the dough in tablespoon-sized drops onto ungreased baking sheets. Bake until golden, about 10 minutes. Cool the pans a few minutes before transferring the cookies to a wire rack to cool completely.

Banana-Pineapple-Yogurt Frosty

▶ SERVES 2

1½ cups nonfat milk or soymilk

1 (6-ounce) container nonfat tropical fruit yogurt

2 medium ripe bananas

1 cup well-drained crushed pineapple

2 teaspoons vanilla extract

2 teaspoons sugar or to taste

Sprinkle of ground nutmeg

1. Combine all the ingredients in the container of a blender and process until smooth.

2. Pour the mixture into a suitable container and chill in the freezer about 30 minutes or until ice forms around the edges of the container. Stir again and serve.

Mango-Ginger Ice

▶ SERVES 4

Juice of 3 large limes
1 tablespoon grated fresh ginger
3 ripe mangoes, peeled and sliced
1 teaspoon fresh lime zest
1 cup sugar syrup (see sidebar)

Combine the ingredients in the container of a blender and process until smooth. Chill the mixture for an hour, then churn according to ice cream maker manufacturer's directions. Scoop the mixture into a container and freeze.

HOW DO YOU MAKE A SIMPLE SUGAR SYRUP?

To make sugar syrup: Combine 3 cups water and 2 cups granulated sugar in a saucepan and cook over medium-low heat until the sugar dissolves entirely and the mixture turns slightly syrupy. Set aside to cool. Save leftovers for another use.

Almond Cornstarch Fruit Pudding

▷ SERVES 4

3 tablespoons cornstarch

2 cups almond-flavored soymilk, divided

2 large egg yolks

½ cup sugar

2 teaspoons almond extract

1 teaspoon vanilla extract

Pinch of salt

2 tablespoons butter

1 cup blueberries

1 cup sliced strawberries

1. In a medium mixing bowl, combine the cornstarch with 3 tablespoons soymilk. Add the egg yolks and sugar and mix to combine. Stir in ½ cup soymilk to make a paste.

2. Heat the remaining soymilk in a large saucepan over medium-low to medium heat and, stirring gently, slowly pour in the cornstarch mixture. Increase the heat to medium-high and bring the mixture to a boil. Immediately reduce the heat to medium-low and, stirring gently, add the almond and vanilla extracts, salt, and butter.

3. Meanwhile, put the fruit into a 2-quart serving bowl. When the pudding mixture is thickened slightly, pour it over the fruit. Let the pudding cool slightly before serving or chill and serve cold.

Nectarine-Cherry Tart with Oat Crumble Topping

▶ SERVES 4-6

2 large ripe nectarines, unpeeled and thinly sliced
2 cups fresh or frozen pitted cherries
1 cup firmly packed brown sugar, divided
3 tablespoons instant tapioca
1 tablespoon plus ¼ cup diced firm butter, divided
1 teaspoon vanilla extract
1 (9") deep-dish pie crust
1 cup old-fashioned rolled oats
1 cup toasted walnut pieces
3 tablespoons flour
¼ cup butter
Heavy cream for topping (optional)

1. Preheat oven to 350°F.

2. In a medium bowl, toss the nectarine slices and cherries together, then add ½ cup brown sugar and tapioca. When this mixture is well combined, add 1 tablespoon butter and vanilla. Spoon the mixture into the pie crust.

3. To make the topping, combine the oats, walnut pieces, ½ cup brown sugar, flour, and ¼ cup butter in a medium bowl and mix well until the topping is crumbly. Sprinkle over the filling and press down.

4. Bake until the crust and topping are brown, about 30 minutes. Serve warm and drizzle each slice with heavy cream if using.

Fruited Blondies

▶ SERVES 9

½ cup (1 stick) unsalted butter

8 ounces white chocolate

¾ cup firmly packed light brown sugar

1 large egg, lightly beaten

1 teaspoon vanilla extract

1 cup white whole-wheat flour

1 teaspoon baking powder

1 teaspoon salt

⅓ cup dried blueberries or more as desired

⅓ cup dried cranberries or dried cherries or more as desired

1. Melt the butter and chocolate together in a double boiler over just-simmering water. When melted, remove from the heat and set aside to cool.

2. Preheat oven to 350°F. Lightly butter an 8" or 9" cake pan.

3. In a medium mixing bowl, beat together the sugar and egg until light and fluffy. Beat in the vanilla.

4. Combine the flour, baking powder, and salt in a separate medium bowl, then add to the sugar mixture and beat until just incorporated. Stir in the butter-chocolate mixture gently and the two different berries until just incorporated. Spoon the batter into the prepared pan.

5. Bake the blondies about 25 minutes or until the center feels firm and a toothpick inserted in the center comes out clean. Cool on a rack before slicing.

Margo's Rhubarb and Pineapple Tart

SERVES 4–6

3 cups chopped fresh or frozen rhubarb

2 cups canned crushed pineapple, well drained

1 cup sugar

2 tablespoons cornstarch

1 sheet frozen puff pastry, thawed

1. Preheat oven to 350°F.
2. Combine the rhubarb, pineapple, sugar, and cornstarch in a large mixing bowl; mix well.
3. On a lightly floured surface, roll out the sheet of puff pastry just enough to fit into a deep 1½-quart baking dish. Press it into the dish and fill it with the fruit mixture. Fold the corners in toward the center.
4. Bake the tart about 40 minutes or until the crust has puffed and turned brown. Serve it hot or still warm.

Chocolate Tofu Pudding

▶ SERVES 4

2 cups nonfat milk or soymilk
1½ cups silken firm tofu
2 (1.3-ounce) boxes sugar-free and fat-free chocolate pudding mixture
1 cup chocolate morsels

1. Combine the milk, tofu, and pudding mixture in a blender and process until smooth. Pour the mixture into a medium saucepan. Heat slowly over medium-low heat, stirring constantly until the mixture thickens.

2. Remove from the heat, stir in the chocolate bits, and pour into a medium heatproof bowl. Chill until ready to serve.

Brazilian-Style Passionfruit Pudding

1 (14-ounce) can coconut milk, well chilled

1 (14-ounce) can sweetened condensed milk

1 (16.8-ounce) bottle passionfruit concentrate

2 cups cubed pound cake

1 cup toasted shredded coconut

Fresh fruits such as cut-up strawberries or blueberries for garnish

> **WHAT IS PASSIONFRUIT?**
>
> A tropical fruit native to Brazil, passionfruit has a subtle sweetness and perfume that only enhances its appeal. Its nectar is often blended into a fruit drink, and a passionfruit concentrate, which you need for this recipe, is readily available at Hispanic markets. You may also find a frozen concentrate, but it does not produce the same results.

1. Carefully scoop out the thick layer of coconut milk and put it into a medium bowl. Beat the milk until it thickens and resembles partially whipped heavy cream. Stir in the condensed milk. Fill the condensed milk can with the passionfruit concentrate and pour it into the mixing bowl. Stir well to combine the milks and juice.

2. Line the bottom of a 2-quart dessert bowl with the pound cake. Pour the passionfruit mixture over top and chill until firm.

3. To serve, sprinkle the toasted coconut over the mousse, spoon the mixture into individual bowls, and garnish with fresh fruits as desired.

Tropical Cheesecake

▶ SERVES 8

2 cups crushed gingersnaps

4 tablespoons melted butter

2 tablespoons grated fresh ginger

2 tablespoons brown sugar

2 pounds cream cheese at room temperature

2 cups granulated sugar or to taste

4 large eggs

2 tablespoons cornstarch

2 teaspoons vanilla extract

Pinch of salt

½ cup shredded coconut

½ cup diced dried papaya

½ cup thinly sliced almonds

1. Preheat oven to 325°F.

2. In a medium bowl, combine the crushed gingersnaps and the butter, then press the mixture into the bottom of a 10" springform pan. Sprinkle the grated ginger and brown sugar on top of the crumbs, pressing them into the crust.

3. In a medium bowl, beat the cream cheese and sugar until smooth. Beat in eggs one at a time until well combined. Add cornstarch, vanilla, and salt. Stir in the fruit by hand.

4. Pour half the mixture onto the crust, sprinkle a layer of almonds on top, and pour on the remaining mixture.

5. Bake at least 1 hour and 20 minutes or until the center is firm; turn off the heat but leave the cheesecake in the oven until it is cool. Then refrigerate it at least 12 hours before slicing.

Berry-Streusel Tart

▶ SERVES 6

1 (16½-ounce) package sugar cookie dough
½ cup all-purpose flour
3 cups fresh or frozen mixed berries
¼ cup granulated sugar
2 tablespoons cornstarch
1 teaspoon almond extract

1. Preheat oven to 350°F. Lightly butter and flour an 8" × 8" or 9" × 9" round or square cake pan.

2. Slice the cookie dough into two portions, using ¾ of the dough for the crust. Press the dough into the bottom of the pan.

3. In a medium bowl, combine the flour and the remaining cookie dough, crumbling the mixture with your fingertips to make a streusel; set aside.

4. In a separate medium bowl, toss the berries with the granulated sugar, cornstarch, and almond extract and spoon the mixture into the pan. Sprinkle the streusel mixture evenly over top.

5. Bake about 40 minutes or until the top has turned brown and the center feels firm. Remove from the oven and eat hot or cold.

Triple-Chocolate Cupcakes

▶ MAKES 16

4 ounces unsweetened chocolate squares
½ pound (2 sticks) unsalted butter
6 large eggs
1 cup granulated sugar
¾ cup cake flour
1½ teaspoons baking powder
2 teaspoons vanilla extract
1 tablespoon cocoa powder
Pinch of salt
1 cup mini chocolate morsels

1. Preheat oven to 350°F. Spray nonstick muffin cups with nonstick cooking spray.

2. In a small saucepan, melt the chocolate and butter together over low heat. When melted, cool to room temperature.

3. Meanwhile, in a large mixing bowl, beat the eggs with the sugar until the mixture turns a pale lemon-yellow. Spoon the cooled chocolate mixture into the sugar-egg mixture and stir until combined. Stir in the cake flour, baking powder, vanilla, cocoa powder, and salt and beat about 30 seconds. Stir in the chocolate morsels. Spoon the mixture into the cups until each is about ⅔ full.

4. Bake 15–18 minutes or until a toothpick inserted in the center comes out clean and the cupcakes feel firm. Cool completely.

Ginger-Tapioca Pudding

▶ SERVES 4

½ cup pearl tapioca soaked in 1 cup
water at least 12 hours

1 cup ginger syrup

1½ cups coconut milk

2 large eggs, well beaten

Pinch of salt

6 coconut macaroons, crumbled

PEARL TAPIOCA

The old-fashioned tapioca pudding called for using the regular, not instant, pearl tapioca made from the starch of the cassava plant. Larger and harder than the instant tapioca pearls, these require soaking at least 12 hours, but preferably for up to 24 hours. Otherwise, they never quite soften during cooking. Despite this advance planning, the pudding is really worth the effort.

1. In a medium bowl, combine the tapioca, ginger syrup, and coconut milk and then pour into a large saucepan. Stir in the eggs and salt and heat over medium-low heat, stirring constantly as the mixture begins to thicken.

2. Meanwhile, sprinkle the crumbled macaroons into the bottom of a 1½-quart dessert dish.

3. When the tapioca pudding has thickened, spoon it into the dessert dish and completely chill until firm.

Ultra Chocolate-Mint Tart

▶ SERVES 6

1 tablespoon vegetable oil

4 ounces semisweet chocolate squares

1 pound cream cheese at room temperature

½ cup unsifted confectioners' sugar plus additional for sprinkling

2 tablespoons cornstarch

2 large eggs

1 tablespoon unsweetened cocoa

1 tablespoon brandy

1 (9") ready-made chocolate cookie crumb crust

½ cup mint-chocolate morsels

1. Preheat oven to 350°F.

2. Combine the vegetable oil and the chocolate squares in the top of a double boiler and melt the chocolate over just-simmering water. Set aside to cool slightly.

3. Meanwhile, in a large bowl, beat together the cream cheese, sugar, and cornstarch until smooth. Beat in the eggs one at a time. Stir in the cocoa, brandy, and melted chocolate. Spoon the mixture into the crust. Sprinkle the top with the mint-chocolate bits.

4. Bake the tart about 1 hour or until the center is firm. Remove from the oven and cool. Before serving, sprinkle with confectioners' sugar.

Peanut Butter Cups

> SERVES 8

½ cup crunchy peanut butter

1 (8-ounce) package soy cream cheese at room temperature

¾ cup packed brown sugar

1 large egg, lightly beaten

3 tablespoons cornstarch

½ cup chocolate morsels

1 (16.3-ounce) tube flaky refrigerator biscuits

1. Preheat oven to 375°F. Spray muffin tins with nonstick cooking spray.

2. Combine the peanut butter, cream cheese, and sugar in a mixing bowl and beat until smooth. Add the egg and cornstarch and beat again. Fold the morsels in by hand.

3. Roll out the biscuits one at a time on a lightly floured surface and fit each into a muffin cup so that it forms a "crust." Spoon the peanut butter mixture into each biscuit crust. Reduce the temperature to 350°F.

4. Bake the muffins 25–30 minutes or until the center feels firm to the touch. Remove from the oven and cool to firm completely.

METRIC CONVERSION TABLE

VOLUME CONVERSIONS

U.S. Volume Measure	Metric Equivalent
⅛ teaspoon	0.5 milliliter
¼ teaspoon	1 milliliter
½ teaspoon	2 milliliters
1 teaspoon	5 milliliters
½ tablespoon	7 milliliters
1 tablespoon (3 teaspoons)	15 milliliters
2 tablespoons (1 fluid ounce)	30 milliliters
¼ cup (4 tablespoons)	60 milliliters
⅓ cup	90 milliliters
½ cup (4 fluid ounces)	125 milliliters
⅔ cup	160 milliliters
¾ cup (6 fluid ounces)	180 milliliters
1 cup (16 tablespoons)	250 milliliters
1 pint (2 cups)	500 milliliters
1 quart (4 cups)	1 liter (about)

WEIGHT CONVERSIONS

U.S. Weight Measure	Metric Equivalent
½ ounce	15 grams
1 ounce	30 grams
2 ounces	60 grams
3 ounces	85 grams
¼ pound (4 ounces)	115 grams
½ pound (8 ounces)	225 grams
¾ pound (12 ounces)	340 grams
1 pound (16 ounces)	454 grams

INDEX

Note: Page numbers in **bold** indicate recipe category lists.

R

Radicchio, grilled, 172
Raisins, in Carrot-Raisin Muffins, 33
Recipes, planning meals with, 11–12, 14
Rhubarb and pineapple tart, 288
Rice and wild rice
    about: to stock, 10
    Lemon-Scented Rice with Fruit Salsa Salad, 88
    Red Pepper Rice with Mushrooms and Sweet
        Peas, 211
    Slow-Cooker Paella, 215
    Slow-Cooker Red Beans and Rice, 217
    Spanish Artichoke and Zucchini Paella, 209
    Stuffed Cabbage, 168–69
    Sun-Dried Tomato Risotto with Spinach and Pine
        Nuts, 208
    Sweet Rice and Sweeter Peppers, 214
    Wild Mushroom Risotto, 216
Rice cooker/steamer, 8
Root vegetables, **133**–56. *See also specific root
    vegetables*
Rutabagas, recipes with, 136, 140, 141

S

Salads and dressings, **71**–90
Salt and pepper, 10
Sauces. *See* Appetizers and sides; Hollandaise
    Sauce; Tomatoes
"Sausage" Bread Pudding, 266
Scones, 40
Seasoning secret, 67
Shelf life of ingredients, 11
Snow peas, recipes with, 160, 203
Sodium intake, swelling and, 75
Soups and stews, **91**–132, 187
Sour Cream Butter Cake, 279
Spinach
    about: sneaking in any dish, 227
    Baked Spinach Tart, 178
    Citrus, Fennel, and Spinach Salad, 79
    Creamed Spinach, 172
    pasta with, 220–21, 222, 227
    Spinach and Feta Pie, 175

Spinach and Tomato Sauté, 158
Spinach Pancakes with Cardamom, 177
Spinach Quiche, 248
Spinach-Stuffed Vegetables, 170–71
Spinach with Pine Nuts (Pignoli) and Garlic, 165
Sun-Dried Tomato Risotto with Spinach and Pine
    Nuts, 208
Tomato, Mozzarella, and Spinach Salad, 82
Vegan Spinach and Artichoke Dip, 45
Spring rolls, 57, 58
Squash
    Acorn Squash Soup with Anise and Carrots, 131
    Clean Creamy Zucchini Soup, 104
    Cumin-Roasted Butternut Squash, 180
    Roasted Asparagus with Mixed Summer Squash
        and Peppers, 199
    Roasted Vegetables, 201
    Spanish Artichoke and Zucchini Paella, 209
    Summer Squash Casserole, 225
    Zucchini Bread, 20
    Zucchini "Lasagna," 193
    Zucchini Ragout, 205
Stocks, 92, 93
Stovetop options and equipment, 8–9
Sugar, 9
Sugar syrup, 284
Sweet potatoes
    about: boiling/baking for nutrition, 121
    Chipotle and Thyme Sweet Potatoes, 154
    Cuban Black Beans and Sweet Potatoes, 151
    Gingered Mashed Sweet Potatoes, 147
    Overly Stuffed Baked Sweet Potato, 155
    Smoky Black-Eyed Pea Soup with Sweet
        Potatoes and Mustard Greens, 118–19
    Spicy Sweet Potato Soup, 121
    Sweet Potato Apple Latkes, 37
    Swiss Chard Rolls with Root Vegetables, 153

T

Tacos, 59, 259
Tapioca pudding, with ginger, 294
Tempeh "Chicken" Salad, 90
Tiramisu, 276
